"*Perspective is a gift...just like this book. Through personal stories, self-deprecating humor and an engaging style, Jon helps us see ourselves for who we really are, and in doing so, opens a door for us to become everything God intends us to be.*" Kevin Fischer, Lead Pastor, Miami Vineyard Community Church

"*Jon Quitt is one of the best communicators I have ever had the joy of listening to. When he shares his heart like he does in this book, it is clear, honest and to the point. Jon very convincingly sounds the trumpet for all of us to get in line with the life Jesus modeled!*" Chris De Wet, Global CEO, AFMIN

"*In a world that pushes towards self-promotion and a "me" mentality this book shows us the truth of God's heart, that our worth would not be found in applause but in the amazing story of God. It is Christ who exalts, and this book helps us to see practically how to "get low" and get out of the way with a true heart of humility as described in scripture.*" Jimmy Bowers, Campus Pastor, Church of the Highlands

"*Jon's new book We're All Heroes in Our Story challenges cultures to go beyond the seductive power of selfies, the endless need to check how many likes I get on a Facebook post and the dread of posting another because it may not get "liked" as much as the last post. Jon's candid, witty and vulnerability draws the reader into unexplored places of where humility isn't revealed and calls us to live a life of Jesus. It's his humility that wins hearts.*" Jon Sterns, Lead Pastor, Franklin Vineyard Church

"*The Scripture is clear that humility is the open door through which the Grace of God is received. Jon Quit has done the body of Christ a service by pointing us to the right path leading to our humility; the Glory of God. He has reminded us in a very readable and even joyful style that as our awareness and appreciation of the Glory increases, in the words of John the Baptist, we decrease. Which is I read Jon's book, I felt the pressure being person, and thus the freedom to worship the* Dan Arsenault, Church For Skeptics

D1516667

STAY LOW!

WE'RE ALL HEROES IN OUR OWN STORY

WE'RE ALL HEROES IN OUR OWN STORY

Jon Quitt

CROSSLINK
PUBLISHING

We're All Heroes in Our Own Story

D
C CrossLink Publishing
www.crosslinkpublishing.com

Library of Congress Control Number: 2016937112

ISBN: 978-1-63357-076-4

TABLE OF CONTENTS

For years my two kids played Upward Basketball at the local megachurch complex. If you're unfamiliar with Upward, it's basically a sports league designed by overprotective parents who think their children should wear helmets when using the toilet. Kids (and parents) are encouraged not to keep score and to make sure to cheer when the other team makes a basket. That idea is generally idiotic. But I digress. At the end of the season, all of the children were lined up (still wearing their helmets and bubble wrap) and they were all declared winners and given a trophy. To be fair, the kids loved it. My kids loved it. But I was insanely angry. There were technically *no* winners, because there were no losers. After the ice cream party and our family was driving home, I couldn't help myself from addressing the obvious lies the coaches had told my children. I knew I needed to set things right.

Now before you label me a terrible parent, please know that I love my children ferociously. They are amazing, sensitive, smart, and fun kids who have a huge destiny attached to their lives. But professional athletes they will never be. Winners at basketball? Not that season. (I did keep score.)

Our children's basketball career ended and we learned a couple lessons.

LESSON #1: people are told they are all winners. Everyone is number one. There is never a person that has to stand at the end of the line. No one is ever wrong. No one lacks ability, skill or prowess. Why? Because everyone is a winner.

I have now spent my fair share of time in school classrooms visiting teachers, and I have found that the same lie my teachers told me has not yet expired. You're familiar with the lie: "Children, every one of you can be the president of the United States. If you put your mind to it, you can do anything."

That's a lie. We know it's a lie. However, it's a nice, affirming, feel-good lie. Still a lie, though. There are twenty-five other children in my thirteen-year-old's class, and they cannot all be the president. Besides the obvious truth that there are twenty-five children and only one position, the lie is still offered. But also the less obvious and less affirming: there are children in my son's class who are not driven enough to battle the political arena. There are children in my son's class who are not smart enough. There is even a child who is not a citizen of the United States ... so legally she cannot be the president. Not everyone can be number one.

We have grown up hearing and believing we are all amazing. We are the heroes of not just our story, but every story. And because we are the hero, that automatically makes everyone else something else—more often the loser, the weakling, or even the enemy. Believing that we are all destined for some sort of public exaltation now puts enormous pressure on our heart to succeed, but also on everyone else to recognize how mind-blowing we really are.

LESSON #2: people lie to us. Of course we already know this to be true. We have been on the receiving end of a lie and it hurts. We have lied and hurt others. But the lie that I'm talking about is different. I'm talking about a subtle lie that warms the heart but sets the receiving person up for an epic fail.

Proverbs 26:28 says, "A lying tongue hates its victims, and a flattering mouth works ruin." In other words, while we want to be stroked and flattered, it only pours poison into our already deceived soul.

We are lied to, but we like it.

This kind of lie is best demonstrated by watching the tryouts of *American Idol* or any other talent show. Suzy Q No-talent grabs the mic and belts out the latest Beyonce song and is told her rendition may have actually injured children back stage. Suzy is indignant because she knows she is the next big star. Why does Suzy believe that? Cause Momma No-talent is a coward and told her daughter every night that she was the best singer in the world and she should chase her dreams of Broadway. What Momma No-talent should have told her daughter is that she certainly is created in the image of God and gifted in significant ways, but singing is not one of those gifts. Instead, Momma lied.

The reason this lie is so palatable is because we want to believe we are amazing. We don't rebuff the lie because we like the lie. We want to believe that we will be the president, a runway model, a megachurch pastor, or at the very least an anonymous millionaire. But a lie is a lie and will always lead us to disaster and far away from God's best.

Perhaps the most dangerous kind of lie is when we lie to ourselves. Because if there is anyone we trust though we shouldn't, it's ourselves (Proverbs 3:5–6). We believe what we tell our heart. We parrot the lie ... "I am a star," "I deserve that promotion," "I belong on that stage," "My wife is lucky to be married to me."

Lies.

To be fair I am not saying every person is not deserving of a promotion or even has the skills to grab the microphone. The issue here is not whether you get promoted or land on the stage. The issue is whether you believe you are entitled to every advantage, advancement, and leg-up because you are God's favorite child.

Seeing ourselves in the light of Jesus and his ferocious love for us changes our expectations.

So how do we transition our lives from believing we are at the center of our personal universe to orbiting around the Creator? How do we fade into the background of life and let Jesus come to the foreground? More specifically, how do we step off our own personal throne and get low?

In the following pages I'd like to talk about your story. And like any great story of the ages it will contain a villain, supporting characters, a plot, personal crisis, and of course a hero. Hopefully you're discovering who the hero is, but personal discovery only comes as you live out your story in light of who is writing the script. Ultimately the premise of this book is that there is only one hero in the narrative of life, and His name is Jesus Christ. His goal in clothing himself with flesh and dying a terrible death and then rising from the dead was not to make you a winner, but to display His splendor and glory for the world. He is the hero of every story, including yours. His goal is that you would show the world how great HE is, not how great YOU are. This is a book about humility. It is not necessarily a HOW-TO book, but we will talk about a few nuts and bolts. Whether a transformative moment happens or not, I hope you begin to see yourself as God sees you. And as that happens, I believe you will be able to do the work of getting low, embracing a life of humility, and letting God take care of the results.

The following pages will be broken into six bite-size portions. Each chapter title is framed in story language. This is done not only to keep it fun, but to remind you that you are in a huge cosmic narrative in which the ending has been written, the villain has already been vanquished, and the hero sits enthroned in praise forever. Obviously, this is not an exhaustive treatise on humility—just the opposite. My hope is that this tool will be easily accessible so that you can be as honest as possible with yourself and God. You're not going to need to hike through the theological wilderness, but you will be asked to walk the journey of faithfulness. You will be confronted with your problem as a broken sinner, Jesus as the great hero, and what it really looks like to joyfully submit to your part of the story of Grace. This is about God and his glorious invitation to you to remember that he is the hero, star and savior of not just your story, but every story.

CHAPTER 1

Your First Chapter of Personal Humility

Nobody is lining up for a good wholesome dose of humility. Be honest for a second. Humility is, well, humbling. It means you don't get the credit. Humility implies choosing to be second or third or 4,128th in line. Getting low looks good on the rack, but nobody wants to try it on. We admire the humble from afar. We encourage it in our children as an admirable quality, but we would trade humility for a full scholarship to Princeton. At the end of the day we think humility is a good idea, but not something worth truly pursuing. It's sort of like exercising. It's a good idea, but I'd rather eat an entire sleeve of Fig Newtons than get on a Stairmaster. Not only are we the fattest nation on the planet, we are the most proud. We say to ourselves, "Sure I'd like to have a healthy dose of humility, but humility is for people without ambition." "Humility is for poor people." Or self-deceptively we say, "I am humble. Why can't you see it, dummy!?"

I was reminded of this during the 2015 NBA finals. Lebron James, unquestionably an incredible player—maybe the best player in the world. But I was blown away by what he said at the press conference after losing to the Golden State Warriors. A reporter asked him if the loss affected his confidence. His response?

"Nah, I feel confident because I'm the best player in the world. It's simple."

Here lies the problem. It's admirable to be excellent in a field or sport. In fact, it's expected that if a person makes millions of dollars as a basketball player, they should hit that three-pointer. But when that player starts believing his own press clippings, we hate them. Outright arrogance angers us.

But let me tell you what happens when we live too long in American Evangelicalism: We hate arrogance in others, but tolerate it in ourselves. We learn the language of humility. We figure out what it looks like to get low, so long as we don't actually have to get low. We regularly use phrases like, "To God be the glory" or "Jesus did it through me," or "I was just a vessel of the Holy Spirit." To be sure those phrases can be real and authentic. But often those words are simply a veneer of humility atop a rotting foundation of pride. What started out as a real experience with the Spirit of God who changes us and lets us see Him for who He really is, the supreme Ruler and merciful Father, often turns into behavior modification at best and pretending at worst. We become like the church at Ephesus who Jesus warns, "You lost your first love." That is, the very person that consumed us, stirred our emotions, and agitated our intellect in the beginning, has now just become an accessory to our life. We're glad Jesus saved us, but at the end of the day it's our life and we're not really interested in Jesus messing with our issues and heart. Somehow we begin to believe once again that we're the hero of the story. And in the honest moments of our heart, we know we don't deserve the preeminence in our lives, but we don't know how to find our way back to humility.

We love humility from a distance. But sooner or later if we want to get low and have Jesus lifted high in our lives, one chapter of our life must end and a new one must begin. The beauty of a new chapter in life is that it's new and fresh, and the possibilities are endless. Sky's the limit! What makes a new chapter in life scary, however, is not knowing the ending. The beauty of your story is that the ending is everything you could dream of, and more. In fact, there is nothing you can do to mess up what has been destined to take place in your life. Jesus has secured your ending before He laid the foundations of the world. If you're wondering about the end, spoiler alert! He wins. Jesus defeats his enemies. He set the captives free. And He sets himself up as king, and creation will marvel at him for eternity. That is *the* ending. And it's the ending that gives us courage to move through our own beautiful plot called life.

As we move forward and pop this inflated ego of ours, let me reaffirm you of the one constant in your story—you win, too! I'm not going to call you a "winner" because I currently don't have a local cable show airing at three in the morning telling people to just believe in their inner awesomeness. You are *not* awesome! But thankfully it has never been your breathtaking splendor that moves you forward. It has always been the humble and ferocious work of Jesus Christ on your behalf. If you have submitted your heart and life to the person of Jesus Christ, you do win. Jesus has taken all the loss, all the guilt, and all the sin of humanity and laid it on himself (Isaiah 53) so you can walk in true freedom and humility that impacts others. Conversely, our sin and rebellion always set us up to lose. When Jesus made the proclamation from the cross, "It is finished," he really meant it. All the work you and I expend in climbing upward is futile because Jesus has done all the work necessary for right standing with our Heavenly Father.

The great exchange of 2 Corinthians 5:21 changes everything. "For our sake he made him to be sin who knew no sin, so that in him we might become the righteousness of God." The sin that is destined to destroy us has been taken by Jesus Christ, and in turn He gives us his righteousness. In simpler terms, Jesus took what we deserved and we got what he deserved. He got the epic loss and we got the win.

In spite of popular teaching, Jesus is not particularly interested in making sure you're number one at work or that you get that raise or that your health is secure. Jesus is supremely interested in magnifying himself as the King as you and I, the residents of his kingdom, glorify him with our lives. That is, God is not most glorified when we achieve greatness, but as we lay our life down and take up his Name. What you will find as God shapes your heart in humility is that in your prayer for advancement up, he may actually take you on the escalator down—because down is the greatest place of honor in the kingdom. Getting low by the world's standards often sets you up to win in the Kingdom of God.

JESUS IS SETTING YOU UP TO WIN

If the Facebook/Twitter/Instagram phenomenon has taught us anything, it's that we want to appear to have our lives put together without actually having to have it together. Take a look at most people's social media pages. Everyone looks amazing—thin, deep tans, and every hair in place. Even their children appear to be strong, loving, and obedient. Never a mention of disappointment or personal frailty. I've yet to see anyone's status read, "Sure am glad my cousin Stu is gettin' out of prison today!" That would be far too real, far too personal. What we do read on our "friends" walls are, by all appearances, that they are living the American dream. Then we see them in Wal-Mart and we do a double take. We think to ourselves, *They've gained some serious weight. And their kids look like they just stepped out of the pages of* Lord of the Flies.

What happened? Nothing happened besides the obvious: they lied—and if not lies, Photoshop. We all post the better version of us. The digital universe continues to tempt us to lay before our peers the self we wish we were, the self we might actually be one day a year, but are far from 364 other days. In honest moments we know we are frauds. Yet the beauty of the cross and the gift of Jesus Christ is understanding that we are now free to be. The performance of trying to be someone, even a better someone, is over. The goal of this life is not to get better or to be more, but to surrender all. Meeting Christ and embracing his love for us is embracing a new identity.

Our identity as Christ followers is rooted in the righteousness of Jesus. This kind of righteousness can only originate from God and is given to us as a gift. Who we will be has changed. We have moved from unrighteous to fully righteous and holy before God. We were an enemy of God. Now we are friends. We were filthy in His sight. Now we are clean. We were rebels involved in a cosmic rebellion. Now we are servants. Our identities have shifted. We *were* the heroes in our own story. Now we see Who the real hero actually is. No longer are we able to think we are bringing anything to the table of God except our own sin and rebellion. The gospel of Jesus sets us free to let God do the heavy lifting of being God. In addition, the revelation that we are utterly dependent on God sets us up to see ourselves for who we really are. However, seeing yourself for who you are is tricky. Our hearts are desperately wicked. So to accurately evaluate ourselves is like trying to shave by a mirror that is fogged up. Since you can't trust yourself, our next go-to are our friends. But we can't really trust them either. Why?

Because they lie to us. I thought we already covered that?!

As much as we are called to walk in deep relationship with people and even allow them to speak life and truth into our lives, we can't confirm or deny our identity on what they think, say, or even believe about us. This is why having a firm identity established in the person of Jesus Christ, his thoughts towards you and the fullness of his grace at work in your life not only will change how you see the world, but will ultimately change how you see yourself.

If the old *Saturday Night Live* sketch of Stuart Smalley sitting in front of his mirror chanting, "I'm good enough, smart enough, and doggone it, people like me!" is even close to how you coach yourself when you are depressed and confused, then your spiritual eyes have cataracts when it comes to seeing who you really are in Christ. You don't coach yourself to be a winner. To be clear, you're not a winner. Jesus Christ is the winner, supremely valuable, and demands every ounce of glory. However, that does not mean you don't have incredible worth and have a destiny attached to your life. Your life, marriage, and even upward mobility has the potential to shine brightly the worth of Jesus Christ. Once you and I begin to see that our worth is not connected at all to getting the credit or the applause, we are well on our way to walking in humility in the story of God.

I CAN'T GET ANY CREDIT?

Like so many college students growing up in the 1990s, I was deeply impacted by the ministry of the Passion Conferences. I remember the first time I heard Louie Giglio speak. I couldn't move. I was enamored. Man-crush? Maybe. But I experienced all the signs that the Holy Spirit was present. Goose bumps? Check. Tears? Check. All noise fades into the background? Check. Matt Redman slowly strumming his guitar? Check. But a lightbulb of epic proportions turned on for me during that time. What I discovered was God was about God's glory. Don't skim over that last sentence too quickly.

God is about God's glory. He is not about you, only.

I later heard men like John Piper, Sam Storms, and JI Packer, and many others talk through this idea. I was wrecked by this truth that the gospel of Jesus Christ was not primarily about me, my comfort, or even my eternal destination. I'm actually a little embarrassed to tell you it took me a few years to grab hold of this very central truth that I am not the point. I really believed that Jesus came into the world for me ... or at least just for me. Now if you're reading this and you just tilted your head a bit in confusion and thought you missed a few sentences cause certainly this guy didn't just say 'God isn't about me.' If that just happened, then my guess is that what you heard growing up in church was this:

> *Jesus loves you.* [true] *Jesus left heaven and clothed himself with flesh to take your sin and shame and guilt on himself.* [true] *The judgment that you deserved, Jesus took for you.* [true] *If there was no one else on planet earth, Jesus would still would have died for you because you are Jesus' prize.* [false]

For clarity, and because I don't want to be labeled a heretic — does Jesus love you? Of course. His love for you is expressed in a million different ways, but most effectively by His willingness to lay down his life on a cross so that your sin would be forgiven.

Romans 5:8 says, "But God shows his love for us in that while we were still sinners, Christ died for us."

Did Jesus leave heaven and come to the earth and take on your sin, shame and guilt? Yep.

1 Peter 2:24 says, "He himself bore our sins in his body on the tree, that we might die to sin and live to righteousness. By his wounds you have been healed."

1 John 2:2 says, "He is the atoning sacrifice for our sins, and not only for ours but also for the sins of the whole world." (NIV)

The punishment that you and I deserve, did Jesus take that, too? Absolutely.

Romans 3:25 says, "For God sent Jesus to take the punishment for our sins and to satisfy God's anger against us. We are made right with God when we believe that Jesus shed his blood, sacrificing his life for us." (NLT)

But what about the tearful closer? This last statement is usually sprinkled in with a terrible story about a bus crash and the majority of your youth group burning in Hell. The southern evangelist would linger on this point … "If you were the only person on the planet, Jesus would have come for you, because the gospel is about you."

It sounds good. It has a ring of authenticity. Unfortunately, it's just not [entirely] true. Stay with me here and ask the real question: if Jesus didn't come for you and for me, what did he come for? If you aren't the center of the universe and the preeminent prize in this world, what is?

Glory Is …

I binge-watched a show on Netflix recently called *Band of Brothers*. I wouldn't necessarily recommend it because of the blood and gore, but nonetheless, it records the storyline of an army unit that fought together during WWII. The show is epic, bloody, and raw. It records the parachute jump into Europe and the battle of the Bulge. It's just good TV. During the opening credits, snippets of interviews from the actual men being portrayed are shown. Richard Winters, who is the main character, recalls a conversation with his grandson about WWII.

"Grandpa, were you a hero in the war?"

Long pause.

"No … but I served in a company of heroes."

I was stunned by that phrase: "I served in a company of heroes." Winters was obviously a man who understood his life was not his own. His existence was for the sake of others, and the glory of victory was to be laid down as someone else's prize. In the same way, when we begin to understand that glory and honor (in everything) is the Lord's, then we are now set free to live extravagantly [and dangerously] because our lives are not really our own. What the glory of God does for us is that it shines a light on our small agendas and puny dreams and gives us new eyes to see the gargantuan nature of God and His mission on earth.

As much as we are impressed with our own success and creativity, it all pales in comparison to the glory of God. Humility is a natural by-product of seeing yourself in right proportion to the universe and the God who created it with a word. To be clear, humility is not low self-esteem. It is not you and I proclaiming, "I'm such a dope. I could never really do anything great!" Humility is understanding that any bit of greatness, success, and upward mobility you have is simply a gift to you to be enjoyed so that in turn, you will trust and worship God more deeply and ascribe him glory.

Let Isaiah 42:8 sink in. "I will not give my glory to anyone." Why won't God give you and me His glory? Surely He isn't stingy with the Shekinah. It has nothing to do with God's generosity. The bottom line is that Jesus is the center of the universe. All things are held together by the Word of His mouth and the strength of His right arm. He is not only where all glory returns, but where all glory is from. However, He is not a glory hound. He isn't insecure and in need of constant praise and reminders of his strength. He doesn't require us to give him glory because He longs for it like an insecure thirteen-year-old. He isn't wondering if someone else out there in the universe is getting more press or has more Twitter followers. He is God. The essence of God is Glory. Glory is not a characteristic of God like His omniscience or his infinitude. Glory is what God is. And what God understands and we forget is that we don't deserve any of the glory because all glory will find its way back to the Creator. So not only will God not give his glory to anyone, it is not ours to have.

Why the short tutorial on the glory of God? Because unless we understand Who is actually first in the universe, we will spend our entire lives pursuing being number one. So the pressure is off! You were never destined to be the center of the universe, and now you can spend your energy and time reflecting the absolute worth of Jesus Christ. His position as the King and absolute ruler of your life now gives you permission to lay down your rights and pursue God's best for you and others. True humility awaits!

CHAPTER 2

The Villain Is Revealed

Every great story must have a villain. Think about your favorite movie. Each storyline contains a beautifully twisted antagonist—an evil and desperate scoundrel whose only role is to undermine and destroy the hero. Don't think Dr. Evil from *Austin Powers*. He's cute and funny—evil but ironic. Think Sauron from *Lord of the Rings*—evil and ferociously dark. Bad guys are necessary for every good story to come to its necessary ending. So I love a good bad guy. Or maybe I hate a bad guy. Either way, my affection for the hero is always stirred against the backdrop of how devilishly dark the villain is.

Our story is no different. The backdrop for our hero is a world drenched in pride. Our world has been overtaken and ruled by the fiercest of adversaries and there is not a lot we can do on our own. Jesus is the hero and our only hope. It's no wonder that when the apostle Peter is coaching new elders, he gives them this advice: "Young men, in the same way, be submissive to those that are older. All of you, clothe yourself with humility toward one another, because, "God opposes the proud but gives grace to the humble." (1 Peter 5:5)

I don't know if you caught that little phrase: "God opposes the proud." Translation? It doesn't matter how talented you are, how gifted you are, or how upwardly mobile you are: when God says he opposes you, it's not gonna go well for you. God opposes the proud, in part because when a person is aligned with pride, they are aligned with our enemy.

Solomon puts it this way: "Pride goes before destruction, and a haughty spirit before a fall" (Proverbs 16:18).

More specifically, there are not a lot of things that God gets angrier over than pride. So much so, He says, "He opposes the proud." Why do you think he opposes the proud? Pride is an inward belief that we are in control—we're pulling the strings and moving the pieces. So we should get the credit. We deserve the glory. And of course, if someone is going to get the applause, it should be us. All the while we're holding up our hands in feigned humility. "No, stop it. I don't deserve it." But inwardly we're lapping it up like dogs.

One of the reasons God opposes this kind of behavior and attitude is because he knows it will never lead to life, only destruction. Because God is out for your best, when he sees pride raise its head in your life, it's like he stands in front of you holding out his hands and says, "Not a step further. I oppose you." The reason he opposes you? Because of whom you're walking with. Often we wonder why it feels like God is holding us back, withholding his favor, when, in fact, he is actually opposing us.

Don't get confused by God's opposition, though. While he may be standing in front of you, keeping you from moving forward, he is also protecting you from a world of hurt and self-centered decisions. Oftentimes when you feel stuck, a well-meaning friend may say to you, "Satan is attacking you because he knows you're succeeding. I'm going to pray and tell Satan to get out of here!"

While I appreciate a friend like that, I'm convinced Satan doesn't really care if you succeed. In fact, he may be the one helping you move up that ladder of success. If he can convince you that real life and satisfaction comes from this world, then he will "help" you as long as you're willing. Once again, God is not opposed to you succeeding. He is opposed to you aligning yourself with anyone (in the natural or supernatural) who will put the spotlight anywhere other than Jesus. God's desire and intent in your life is that you would move towards greater submission and humility in your life. When God opposes you, it is actually an act of love and concern for you. He may remove people, jobs, and even health in your life so that you will learn to joyfully submit to Jesus.

WE'RE DUMB

Don't read that subtitle and get offended. Just own it. We are dumb people. Sin makes us stupid, and the enemy capitalizes on it. That's not to say we aren't fiercely intelligent and hungry for knowledge. You may have spent years honing a skill or cultivating your education. But have you noticed how often you choose something in spite of the fact that you know it is not good for you? I'm not talking about that extra slice of chocolate cake that will go straight to your waist. I'm talking about decisions that impact your marriage and purity and integrity. We have full knowledge of what is good and will bring glory to God and then we often do the opposite. Yep. We're dumb—it's just true. This is why Isaiah describes us as sheep. "We all like sheep have gone astray. Each of us have turned to [our own way]." Sheep, in spite of loving their shepherds, are dumb. Don't misunderstand me. Sheep are valuable and keen in their own ways. They are generous with affection. Sheep are amazing animals. But they're dumb. And this is why we are described that way. We know what is good for us and yet we continue to choose what is destructive. We can see terrible habits and sinful behavior in others, but we readily choose them for ourselves when no one is looking.

This is why pride is so deadly—because we are so dumb. If I've hurt your feelings, how about I say you just lack self-awareness … dummy! More specifically, our enemy knows our spiritual IQ is somewhere around a 31, and he regularly capitalizes on that. Unfortunately, our idiocy makes us the last people to see pride in our lives. You'd think something so dangerous and deadly would cause us to be on high alert—but we're dumb AND blind. Of course, you and I lack no vision in seeing pride in other people. But pride accomplishes its mission in *your* life by blinding *you* to transformational truth. So you will see other people and be able to identify their sin and brokenness, but will be completely blinded to your own. Pride is the bread and butter of the professionally religious and the calling card of the enemy.

TOOLS OF THE TRADE

The enemy of our soul is intent on shaping our hearts into rebellion by whatever means necessary. Pride, arrogance, haughtiness—whatever you want to call it—comes in all sorts of shapes, sizes, and shades. Do you remember the little joke we used to tell as kids, "What's grosser than gross?" I'm not at liberty to give you any of the punch lines, but I've heard a few that would turn your stomach. But do you know what is grosser than gross? Pride is gross to God. And the two primary kinds of pride are exaltation and self-hatred. The devil and his cohorts will use these subtle forms of pride to help camouflage the darkness building in your soul.

Self-Exaltation is pride that sets you up as the winner, champion, and glory-giver. Gideon and Old Testament Saul both gave themselves over to this kind of pride later in their lives as they set up statues of themselves. This kind of pride is nauseating to be around and it's easy to spot. At the same time, this kind of pride is culturally allowed because it often follows great exploits and incredible skill. This is the Achilles heel of a winner. We're typically not going to see self-exaltation in a kid that gets cut from his middle school basketball team, but we will see it often in the NBA All-Star player. Unfortunately, we excuse this kind of pride in America because we value achievement and success above all things.

However, self-exaltation is a tricky sin. It is hard to identify and nail down in ourselves. The reason is we just assume everyone talks about themselves. We assert, "I'm just making conversation. Sure, it happens to be about me, but that's how dialogue works, right?" But because our hearts are shady, most of what come out of our mouth that happen to be about us are designed so that we might receive a little bit of praise. We long for a pat on the back. Our fractured hearts are thirsty for someone to say we deserve the glory.

For example, humblebrags are now commonplace. Urban Dictionary defines *humblebrag* as, "When you, usually consciously, try to get away with bragging about yourself by couching it in a phony show of humility." Humblebrags make perfect 140-character declarations about our amazing humility! Tweets will sound something like, "I'd like to ask all my friends how I actually got into Harvard. I think they got it wrong! #notsmart." Do you notice the self-effacement? But don't miss the part about Harvard. Or, "I lost 23 lbs. But my husband still looks better! #hottie." Humblebrags are now regular parts of our speech and behavior as believers. We want to be the center of attention and we're just not patient enough for other people to notice our awesomeness. A nudge in the right direction never hurt anyone, right?

If that were true, why does Solomon pen these words in Proverbs 27:2, "Let another praise you, not your own mouth; a stranger, not your own lips"? It's not that praise is a wicked thing. Not at all! Our souls were made, in some distinct way, to long for and receive praise. Often our problem is the kind of praise we long for. If the kind of affirmation we seek is based on our performance, work ethic, or even spiritual activity, then we have drifted into self-exaltation. But if the praise of others reminds us that we are simply conduits of grace, then the praise of others will then stir our hearts to worship God.

Self-hatred is also a form of pride. Self-hatred sets you up as the loser, victim, and glory-stealer. You have undoubtedly met people who suffer from self-hatred. They literally dislike everything about themselves. They complain about their weight, height, skin, personality, communication skills, opportunities, and even about how negative they are. What appears as a person who is overly critical is really just a person exhibiting the symptom of pride. Have you noticed this kind of person always has a worse story that trumps your bad story? "Oh, you fell down the stairs? Yeah, that's bad. But I fell down the stairs into a meat grinder!" "You had a bad haircut? Well, I got cancer and my hair fell out!" "Your wife left you? My wife died!" To be sensitive here, I'm not demeaning seasons of pain. What I'm pointing out is when we find our identity in our terrible experiences, we fall prey to pride. Our circumstances are simply that ... circumstances. Our circumstances will change and always be in flux. However, if our value, identity, and language are defined by the flow of life, our lives will settle into some kind of self-hatred.

This kind of pride is also a bit hard to nail down. It's easy to spot the person who simply hates themselves and wants everyone else to recognize how grotesque they are. But what about the person who is put together on the outside, but on the inside believes that they just don't belong? There is a fairly new psychological phenomenon called Imposter Syndrome. Imposter

Syndrome is when "people are unable to internalize their accomplishments. Despite external evidence of their competence, those with the syndrome remain convinced that they are frauds and do not deserve the success they have achieved. Proof of success is dismissed as luck, timing, or as a result of deceiving others into thinking they are more intelligent and competent than they believe themselves to be." MIT advisors find that many students who are accepted into the prestigious school wonder if the university made a mistake.

Interestingly, self-exaltation and self-hatred share one thing in common—you and I are at the center. Life is still about us. We're either the winner or we're the loser. But, either way, it's about us. Whether life is about you at the top or it is about you at the bottom, it is still about you. And when life is about you, it is never really about God and His glory.

CHAPTER 3

Supporting Characters

So far the hero has been introduced, the villain is in place, and now, like in any great narrative, supporting characters step into the story. Before we move on any further, I think it's worth noting that I'm a Trekkie. Yep, I love Star Trek. I mean, I've never been to a convention where everyone is dressed up like Mr. Spock. And I'm not fluent in Klingon (yet!), but I have seen every movie, watched every episode of all the franchises, and for full disclosure, looked at the prices of tickets for the nearest Trekkie convention. Of course, I omitted all this information while courting my wife. But that's neither here nor there. If you have ever seen an episode of the original Star Trek with William Shatner, you are aware of "the curse of the random-landing party member." Every episode plays itself out in the same way. The Starship Enterprise finds a new life form on a class 7 planet and Kirk orders a landing party to investigate. The landing party includes Kirk, McCoy, Spock, and of course, an unnamed guy who I'll call Ensign Unlucky. Pretty much every episode the person who gets shot, eaten, or dismembered by an alien that looks less like Alf and more like a man in a green garbage bag is Ensign Unlucky. This very important character does serve an important purpose, though—they set an example of what not to do. They are the anti-example.

The same is true in our story. God has certainly put people in your life who serve as glowing examples of moronic idiocy. They carry pride as a trophy. They wear arrogance as a tailored suit. But no matter how they dress up this heinous sin, it still stinks to high heaven. They will come in and out of your life in consistent regularity and they are those whom Solomon plainly calls "fools." Think about the "great cloud of witnesses" mentioned in Hebrews 12 whose purpose is to cheer you on in this race of faith. The "great cloud" are men and women who finished well. They finished the race in which Jesus wins. Now, think about the exact opposite when I say the word "fool." They are men and women who are trying to convince you that the shortcut is the right decision. They will show you well-worn paths that are roads to destruction. Fools unknowingly reflect for us a potential future—a painful future in which poor circumstances have less to do with chance and more to do with arrogance put on display. These people are often our brother-in-laws, a coworker, or even a spouse. Sometimes, and I pray this is not true, but sometimes you are that person to others. The great news is that you don't have to remain that person!

While you wait for the neighborhood idiot to show up and show you how not to live, grab a bible and see a few examples for yourself. As you open the scriptures, please understand that while all scripture is God-breathed and is useful for teaching, rebuking, correcting and training, not all scripture immediately applies. Much of the Scriptures are descriptive in nature. These texts simply show us what happened in history, how men make much of themselves and how God then responds. In contrast, much of the Scriptures are also instructional in nature. Instructional texts are weighted with commands—dos and don'ts. They show us why it is beneficial to obey. While we learn and grow from both descriptive and instructive texts, how we process them are incredibly different. For example, when reading about God destroying entire people groups in the Old Testament, we should not read that and ask, "Okay, how do I apply this? What people group do I want to annihilate?" That would be a bad move. God, in his supreme wisdom and role as judge, could raise up nations and exterminate them with a word. However, we can learn a great deal from watching history from a distance. You and I will see that God has raised up men and women in the bible who are such train wrecks spiritually and emotionally that they end up being anti-examples. Consider these men…

UZZIAH

King Uzziah doesn't get a lot of press these days, but he was quite a king in his time. In fact, the majority of his tenure as king over Judah was filled with success and prosperity. Read this carefully:

> *Uzziah was sixteen years old when he began to reign, and he reigned fifty-two years in Jerusalem. His mother's name was Jecoliah of Jerusalem.* *⁴ And he did what was right in the eyes of the Lord, according to all that his father Amaziah had done.* *⁵ He set himself to seek God in the days of Zechariah, who instructed him in the fear of God, and as long as he sought the Lord, God made him prosper.* (2 Chronicles 26:3–5)

Just for clarity, God prospered his leadership because he did what was right in the eyes of God. This is classic language of humility. He understood the kingdom of God was ruled by a King and the King was God. Let's read some of his accomplishments.

He went out and made war against the Philistines and broke through the wall of Gath (v. 6). Moreover, Uzziah built towers (v. 9). Moreover, Uzziah had an army of soldiers, fit for war (v. 11). And Uzziah prepared for all the army shields, spears, helmets, coats of mail, bows, and stones for slinging (v. 14). In Jerusalem he made machines, invented by skillful men (v. 15). And his fame spread far, for he was marvelously helped, till he was strong (v. 15).

So far, so good. Uzziah begins as a wise king and successful leader. He was being "marvelously helped" by God because he sought Him and humbled Himself before Him. Everything a king would want to accomplish was happening. This is a poignant story of God honoring someone who knows life does not orbit around them but God. Unfortunately, Uzziah's life doesn't end well. After a long season of success, Uzziah began to believe his own press. He assumed he was building a legacy for Israel and for his own fame. Most disappointing, he began to hope that people would remember his name! Watch what happens.

But when he was strong, he grew proud, to his destruction. (v. 16)

It's interesting how the writer connects Uzziah's strength to his destruction. His perceived power led to his own downfall, which included leprosy, living in isolation, and dying with a fractured reputation. Not exactly ending well. Pride truly was his downfall and destruction. I have to wonder, though, what would have happened if Uzziah had just stayed low, trusted the Lord, and been satisfied with Him getting the credit?

SAUL

If Saul desired anything in his reign as king, then it was that he longed for a personal legacy. Unfortunately, it appears Saul had the deck stacked against him from the beginning. Israel, in its desire to be like the surrounding nations, asked for an earthly king. God warned them, perhaps even pleaded with them, but ultimately relented to their request. Saul was chosen. He is recorded as standing a head above all other Israelites. He's a warrior. A gifted leader. This guy is a stud. Truly, he was the [natural] choice to lead this budding nation.

And yet, like so many great leaders, we get the impression that Saul knew he was pretty hot stuff. Leading out of his natural strength created a disaster for himself and the nation he was leading. By 1 Samuel 15, it's recorded that the Lord regretted making Saul king. That statement should carry some weight as we read it. When God "regrets" doing something, it's got to be pretty bad. And why did God regret making Saul King? Pride. It was this sin that turned God's stomach and set Him to make enormous changes in Israel's leadership.

As a result, God removes his presence from Saul and a new king was anointed. This is where the story gets interesting; Saul has been warned that God will remove his presence from His life because pride has put him on the chopping block. And yet what does Saul do? You would think begging God would be in order, but Saul doesn't beg. Instead he has a statue built to commemorate himself. Instead of getting low and repenting, he continues to shore up his reputation. This is what happens to those whose pride becomes their downfall—they build monuments to themselves. They create structures that will remind others of their position and value. Saul carried the title of king, but that was all he had—a title. A person who embraces humility doesn't really care about titles. She's not interested in getting credit. He doesn't ever have to get his way. These kinds of people love for Jesus to be the center and to receive all of the attention. Those who live a lifestyle-of-low have decided that Jesus' reputation is all that matters.

PETER

It's one thing to be humble and something entirely different to be humbled. Peter learned humility only after he was humbled. Many contend that the defining moment in Peter's life was when he confessed Jesus as the Messiah, the coming King of the Jews. While this was a paramount experience for Peter because he received his new name and powerful calling to partner with God, the defining moment for him really came later.

Luke 22 paints the funny scene for us. The disciples are jockeying for position in Jesus' new kingdom. In no uncertain terms they want to know who will get to reign with him in power and glory. And Peter, not to be outdone by the others, says, "Lord, I am ready to go with you to prison and to death." In other words, "I'm in this to the end if that's what it takes." Peter didn't receive the praise he was expecting from Jesus. Instead Jesus gave him an agonizing sneak peak into the future. Before the rooster crowed, Peter was told, he would deny Jesus three times. You may have read the account of Peter's apostasy and remember what happened after the third denial.

Then Peter remembered the word the Lord had spoken to him: "Before the rooster crows today, you will disown me three times." And he went outside and wept bitterly. (Luke 22:61–62, NIV)

Peter's arrogance was born out of a good motive. He desired to prove to Jesus what he was willing to do for the sake of the kingdom. He was willing to die for Jesus! The problem with trying to prove something to Jesus is that it causes us to believe that our striving and our performance are actually worth something. Jesus didn't need anything from Peter. He wasn't looking for proof. Peter had already been chosen. He had already been given a new name. So what was there to prove? That was the moment in which Peter was to be humbled. And boy, was he humbled!

DON'T BUY INTO AMERICAN LEGACY

Let the anti-examples of these three men serve as signposts on your journey. There is this belief that has snuck into American evangelicalism that says, "Leave a legacy. Don't let people forget that you made a difference in this world!" While this sentiment feels right, it's just not Jesus-centric. Solomon understood this when he penned,

> *"No one remembers the former generations, and even those yet to come will not be remembered by those who follow them." (Ecclesiastes 1:11, NIV)*

Think about it. Can you even think of the name of your great, great, great grandmother? Probably not. Let alone, can you think of one way she impacted the world? Again, probably not. But that's okay. A legacy has less to do with having people remember you and more to do with people remembering Christ and his work. The apostle John knew this well when he wrote,

> *"For He must increase. I must decrease."* (John 3:30)

John's words are a pointed reminder for those of us who would like to make a name for ourselves by doing great things for God. The season of celebrity Christians has done much harm to what it truly means to do something significant for God. We have begun to believe that going big with God means WE are big (and loud, influential, and popular). IMPORTANT doesn't always equal BIG. Sometimes the greatest thing you will do in this life will never be known by another human being. Significance can never be measured by the affirmation of others. The moment our metric is based on notoriety, acceptance, or support is the moment we have chosen the path of the anti-example.

THE MOST HUMBLE MAN ... EVER!

Now Moses was a very humble man, more humble than anyone else on the face of the earth. (Numbers 12:3, NIV)

That little verse doesn't get a lot of time in the pulpits of America. Moses, like so many other men and women we read about in the scriptures, were humble. But the question is: what led to their deeply humble stature? Moses, the man who led the nation of Israel out of Egypt after hundreds of years of slavery, is also a man with severe anger issues and with a back-talking bent. While Moses was the instrument God used to free the nation of Israel from Pharaoh, it wasn't because Moses was strong, influential—or humble. Then what about that whole Moses was "more humble than anyone on the face of the earth" business?

Our tendency as readers of the bible is not only to make ourselves the hero, but also to think the best of all of our biblical forefathers. Time gives way to magical thinking. We tend to forget all their brokenness and highlight their strengths. For example, we know David had an affair with a woman named Bathsheba and later had her husband killed. But David was a man after God's own heart. We know Peter denied Jesus three times—but he also walked on water! And Moses ... we know he killed an Egyptian, argued with God, crumbled under the pressure of leadership— but he was sooooo humble. I think our tendency is to reverse the order of effect. We tend to believe that God chose David because he was a man after God's own heart. Or God appointed Peter because he had faith to walk on water. And Moses was the perfect candidate because he was the most humble man on earth. Could it be we have it backwards? The reason David was a man after God's own heart was because he experienced the tender discipline of the Lord and drank in His mercy when he deserved judgment. The reason Peter was invited out onto the water was not because of his faith, but because of the power of Jesus to lead. And the reason Moses was able to lead the throng of Israel through the Red sea was not because of his humility, but because of God's faithfulness to hear the cries of His people.

If this reversal is true, then how did Moses become such a humble man? We assume he was already humble and that is the reason God chose him. But watch this:

When Moses entered the tent, the pillar of cloud would descend and stand at the entrance of the tent, and the LORD would speak with Moses. And when all the people saw the pillar of cloud standing at the entrance of the tent, all the people would rise up and worship, each at his tent door. Thus the LORD used to speak to Moses face to face, as a man speaks to his friend. (Exodus 33:9–11)

Wow! Moses met with God face-to-face. I don't know about you, but I don't regularly meet with God face-to-face. To meet with God in that way must be terrifying. I think back to the last scene in *Indiana Jones: Raiders of the Lost Ark* when the guy's face melts off when coming in contact with the holiness of God. Try to get that picture out of your mind next time you're having a quiet time with God. But when confronted with the holiness of God and His preeminence, a good face melting may be in order.

For whatever reason, though, God chose to meet with Moses in this very distinct way (and no face melting). He had not, and has not, met with someone like that since. We don't know why but, in His sovereignty, he decided to give Moses this privilege. What becomes increasingly obvious is that Moses' humility was forged in that tent of meeting. Not before and not after. Moses was the most humble man on the face of the earth because he was the only one who had seen God face-to-face and lived. There must be something about the proximity to the glory of God that puts a man in his place.

CHAPTER 4

The Plot

Every story has a plot. The plot is the reason for the story. Nobody likes a story about nothing, unless of course it's *Seinfeld*. The characters and action of every narrative all revolve around a single idea. The single idea, the plot of our own narrative, is the glory of God. But what happens when the plot of our story doesn't go where we want it?

My favorite show of all time is *24*. I love Jack Bauer. If you've never jumped on the Bauer train, it's not too late. All eight seasons are on Netflix ready for your click and binge. *24* was the one hour a week in which we watched every second of Jack's day as he saved the world from a dirty bomb in NYC. It was fascinating. But somewhere around the second season, my wife insightfully asked, "Does he ever go to the bathroom?" So we began to watch. He never took a pee break. Never! And then we trolled some internet bulletin boards and it turns out that was a question people were asking. People wanted to know how he IS "holding it" for a whole day. But let's be honest, sitting on the pot is not good TV. It's just gross. But not every story has a Jack Bauer at the center. Most stories lag. There are layers in which the dialogue feels flat and the action sequences have disappeared. It's the plodding of the characters towards their destiny. The lull is the protagonist's grit to keep moving forward. Often the movement of the storyline is boring and slow. But it's in this middle section of the story where most of the work is done. Lulls are a reality and even a necessity in every story.

In the same way, the quest for humility is found in the quiet, unhurried pace of our life. When all emergencies have passed, relationships have calmed, the work of humility and the plodding of faith happens. While pride is intrinsic to our humanity and can grow quickly into full narcissistic behavior, humility is developed over a lifetime. We must plod, slowly but surely, in the direction of personal anonymity. That is not to say, we don't want to be known in community, we just don't want to get the attention that is not ours. We are not naturally humble people, but as followers of Jesus, having access to the grace of God, we must pursue humility, embrace it, and make war on its behalf.

The church (and I love the church) has moved away from this central theme of personal growth and sanctification. Humility just isn't sexy. The church is much more likely to celebrate a person's gifting, ministry success, and positive behavior than to celebrate the man or woman who serves behind the scenes and demonstrates a quiet perseverance and faithfulness to the Lord. Just look around. When was the last time your church celebrated the single mom or widow who has cared for the bed babies in your church nursery? Unfortunately we are more enamored with upwardly mobile Christians than the incessantly faithful. Because of this trend, humility is not even on the radar for most believers and rarely celebrated.

In fact, because humility is not something we can measure, it feels pointless to pursue it. It's not like you can look back on the last thirty days and say, "Yep, I'm 1.4 times more humble than I was in June." "I performed forty-one acts of meekness this quarter." It doesn't really work that way. The counterintuitive nature of humility is that if you are focusing on being more humble, it can (though not always) turn into a behavior that looks holy and meek on the outside, but is bubbling with self-righteousness on the inside. This is why we see Jesus primarily going after people's hearts first and then their behavior. If our hearts are still in rebellion to Jesus' Lordship and mission, our behavior will always be secondary.

CRAWLING INTO HUMILTY

What does it actually look like to get low, lay down our rights, and somehow not forget Jesus is still in charge? Because a life of humility is developed over a lifetime, God will use everything in our life and circumstances to give us opportunity to get low. Read Apostle Paul's commands and then his subsequent description of Jesus' humility.

Do nothing from selfish ambition or conceit, but in humility count others more significant than yourselves. (command) ⁴ Let each of you look not only to his own interests, but also to the interests of others. (command) ⁵ Have this mind among yourselves, which is yours in Christ Jesus, ⁶ who, though he was in the form of God, did not count equality with God a thing to be grasped, ⁷ but emptied himself, by taking the form of a servant, being born in the likeness of men (description)⁸ And being found in human form, he humbled himself by becoming obedient to the point of death, even death on a cross(description). ⁹ Therefore God has highly exalted him and bestowed on him the name that is above every name, ¹⁰ so that at the name of Jesus every knee should bow, in heaven and on earth and under the earth, ¹¹ and every tongue confess that Jesus Christ is Lord, to the glory of God the Father. (Philippians 2:3–11)

According to the Scriptures, the result of humility is considering other people more significant than us. In addition, a humble heart will quit trying to get ahead. These are difficult and weighty commands. What we discover in this process is that no one accidently becomes humble. You don't stumble into a long-term attitude of self-sacrifice.

Conversely, life continues to roll on with or without our participation. Our job, as it relates to life, is how we will respond to it. My personal theology contends that there are no accidents. Literally, EVERYTHING happens for a reason and by the hand of God. He is in control of every detail of the universe. Does that mean that when you spilled that cup of coffee this morning, "by accident," it was not really an accident? Was it perhaps an angel who tipped it over so that you would be delayed and not get in a tragic car accident, so that one day you could lead your coworker to Christ? I don't know … maybe. But don't be stupid here. My point is simply this: God is in charge. And if God's primary goal in the universe is that He would be exalted and receive all the glory in your life, then He will put you in a position for just that! God receives the greatest glory when our lives reflect his immeasurable worth. So while our job is to respond to what happens to us in life, our job really is to respond to God. As God is moving the pieces of life, pulling the strings of circumstances and leveraging the work of the enemy for our good, he is developing humility in us. What does that look like?

SUCCESS

I have pastored the same church for twelve years. My wife Amy and I started the church in our home as a small group bible study. We invited our neighbors into our home to eat and have conversations around the bible. Within a year fifty people were cramming into our home every Tuesday night. It was exciting in those days because we had no overhead, no building, no staff and, honestly, no expectation. We were just thrilled that people were coming to faith in Christ, growing in their relationship with other believers, and starting to think globally. And then it went sideways. The worst thing for my soul happened—we grew. We started a public service and 100 people showed up. I know that number isn't impressive, but to a twenty-eight-year-old with almost no ministry experience, I was beginning to think, *Wow, I'm pretty amazing!* So we kept meeting and more people showed up and then a few more. We did have a few setbacks the first few years, though. Pockets of people would leave, usually together. And I would say something either really spiritual like, "Well, God is simply refining us. They were the dross and we're the pure gold." Or I would say something really snarky like, "Don't let the door hit you on the way out!" Sometimes I would use both responses at the same time because not only am I deeply spiritual, but I can also be a real jerk. But then more people would come and fill their seats. After a few years things were humming along nicely. Bank accounts were full, the church was on mission, staff was hired. Dang, I was good! Both my wife and I were very pleased with our success. But it wasn't enough.

We didn't understand; this is exactly what we were after, but I would come home on a Sunday after an amazing service, new faces everywhere, and I would think, *Is this it?* I knew something was broken in my heart.

The thing about success is that our metrics are usually all wrong. Meaning, what we're counting is not usually what counts. And when we get what we want, it never really satisfies us the way we thought it would. In addition—and this is when it gets dangerous for our souls—when we succeed (however you define success), we begin to believe that we are truly experiencing the favor of God in our lives. "Praise God! I know my business is booming because of God's hand in my life." "My marriage is solid. It's just the Lord." "I keep getting promotions. Glory!!" To be fair, when you and I succeed, it is God. God is not diametrically opposed to you advancing in your career, making more money, and having greater influence. What he is opposed to, however, is when you do advance in your career, make more money, and have greater influence and then forget that life and your money aren't really about you. Sometimes the worst thing that can happen to you is for you to get everything you want. Success has the potential to derail your faith and keep you entrenched in deep pride that will set you up for unparalleled spiritual failure. This is why the apostle Paul told Timothy,

"But those who desire to be rich fall into temptation, into a snare, into many senseless and harmful desires that plunge people into ruin and destruction." (1 Timothy 6:9)

The implication is that success, or more specifically the pursuit of success, can drive people to destruction. In fact, Paul nails this thought home by saying, "It is through this craving that some have wandered away from the faith and pierced themselves with many pangs." (v. 10)

However, success can also be a beautiful gift of God, ironically, to keep us low and grounded in the reality of the Kingdom of God. If humility is used to shine a light on the greatness and worth of Jesus Christ, success can be a blunt force tool for that very purpose. Think through this: while the majority of culture is impressed with success and wealth, when a person is driven by the glory of God they will say, "Don't be impressed with my success. This is nothing. I don't find my worth in this anymore. It's just money. It's just stuff. I used to chase after it and I came up empty. My worth and value is found in Jesus Christ. He is my everything! He is where real life is found!" What this person has done is becoming a missionary to the successful. This is true incarnational living. A successful man or woman has the ear of other successful men or women. Not only do they understand where they are living, but they understand their greatest need. A humble and successful person is hard to find. But when they are found, you will see many others around them finding faith and fulfillment in Jesus.

If you are already successful or if you are pursuing success and your desire is to give glory to God, get low and shine a bright light on Jesus' worth, you must do a few things.

First, thank God that he has providentially put you in this position. Acts 17:26 says, "From one man he made all the nations, that they should inhabit the whole earth; he determined the times set for them and the exact places they should live." In other words, you are not in a place of influence by accident. God placed you there.

Secondly, repent of your arrogance and belief that somehow you are the reason for your achievement. To be fair, thinking that we are not somehow responsible for our success is incredibly difficult. Given a moment to ponder on this, you will begin to think about all the sacrifices YOU have made, all the weekends spent researching and the nights burning the candle at both ends. Repenting of your arrogance does not mean somehow that you did not work hard. It simply means you don't look at your hard work as the determining factor for your success. Paul understood this well when he said this, "But by the grace of God I am what I am, and his grace toward me was not in vain. On the contrary, I worked harder than any of them, though it was not I, but the grace of God that is with me." (1 Corinthians 15:10) Paul attributed his influence to the grace of God and, by that same grace, he worked incredibly hard.

Third, ask how God would use your success and resources to bring more attention to Jesus. Find out how you can bring greater glory to Jesus Christ with your stuff, money, cars, influence, business, and marriage. Don't forget, this life isn't about you. Don't buy into your own press. You're not that awesome. Jesus, however, is awesome, and he has put you in a place of influence so that others will see Him, not you.

FAILURE

I got beat up. Not recently, but when I was fifteen. I was in the mall and got beat up by a boy I went to school with. Not some verbal lashing, but a straight up punch in the face that knocked me down. My friend who was with me in the food court just watched and waited to see if he would get beat up, too. It was traumatic for me. I had only known love and respect, even a bit of popularity, up until this point in high school. Now I would be the butt of the campus gossip. I was humbled.

Failure is a gateway God uses for our humility. Let's face it—nobody likes to lose. Coming in last embodies everything it means to be a failure. This is the very reason we run from failure like a kid runs from the school bully. What we tend to forget, or maybe you've never learned it, is: failure is not the enemy. While we can give a nod to that truth, most of us don't live that way. We like winners. No, we love winners. As pastor and author Rich Nathan recounts, "You never see the losing team in the locker room saying, "We just give God all the glory for that loss." But why not? Why can't we ascribe God glory not only in our wins, but also in our losses? In fact, it seems that in God's plan for our humility and His glory, he will prepare abundant opportunities for you and me to fail. You read that right—God has and will orchestrate moments for you to come in last.

Why would God allow—or more specifically, cause—you to come in last? Why would God orchestrate a failed business or short-circuit a ministry venture? The short answer is so that you can show the world that God is where your worth and value is found. You see, God knows how to measure "the wins" in your life. A win for you may be a successful business, but the real win for God is when your business fails and you still ascribe worth and value to Him. And even more, "the win" is when others witness this moment of worship and "give glory to their father in heaven." (Matthew 5:16)

Think about the last time in your life it felt like God took something away from you. Maybe it was an opportunity, maybe it was a friendship, maybe it was your job. Perhaps what God was doing was creating MORE opportunity for you. I know that doesn't make sense at first. How can God create more opportunity for me by taking away what I already have? Listen to what Jesus said in John 15, ""I am the true vine, and my Father is the gardener. ² He cuts off every branch in me that bears no fruit, while every branch that does bear fruit he prunes..." (vv.1–2). Not only will Jesus cut off braches that bear no fruit, but the branches that DO bear fruit he prunes or trims them back. That seems cruel until you read why:

"So that it will be even more fruitful."

Jesus will take an already healthy and even fruitful life and he will prune it back. The reason he prunes is not because he is unhappy with you. On the contrary! Jesus removes parts of your life so that your life can be even more fruitful.

Often, what seems like a season of failure for you and me is only a precursor to a season of fruitfulness. And the fruit that Jesus is looking for is not only fruit that will last (John 15:16), but fruit that is born out of seeing Jesus as your greatest worth. This is why failure is such a gift to us. When everything in your life gets removed, that may be the moment you truly see Jesus as enough for you. We will be able to echo what Job said, "Though he slay me, I will hope in him"; (Job 13:15) If you have experienced a season of failure, use these handles to get low and make much of Jesus:

First, thank God for your failure. This may seem like a strange thing to thank God for, but if God is working in every detail of your life, then you can thank Him that he is at work to accomplish His heart and will even in the darkest of times. The apostle James gives us this instruction, "Count it all joy, my brothers, when you meet trials of various kinds, ³ for you know that the testing of your faith produces steadfastness. ⁴ And let steadfastness have its full effect, that you may be perfect and complete, lacking in nothing." (1:2–4) As you are thanking God for this shortfall in your life, your prayer of faith makes you aware that you will lack for nothing when you trust God in your failure.

Secondly, ask God what you need to learn through this failure. Oftentimes the reasons for our failure are difficult to discern. Perhaps you opened a new business and you just can't understand why it never got off the ground. As the dust settles, God may reveal to you that you need to receive more training in management or a deeper understanding in cultural spending trends. Is God that interested in making sure you're prepared? Of course! He is a God who loves it when we pursue excellence. Don't just assume this difficult season was the devil's fault. It is also possible that your failure is a result of the discipline of the Lord. This may seem harsh, but don't forget that God only disciplines those whom He loves (Hebrews 12:6). Because he is eternally wise and also completely loving, he may have removed you from a place of upward mobility because while you were moving up, your heart was actually moving away from Him. Because His intention and what your heart longs for is that you would walk in deep communion with Him, this kind of discipline, though painful at the time, is incredibly loving.

Lastly, learn to boast in your failure so Jesus will be exalted in it. "Just walk it off." That is the advice I give to my kids when they fall. "You'll be fine. Get up." While this may be OK advice to my fourteen-year-old on the tennis court, it is not wholistic for a man or woman seeking to glorify God in all their failures. To be fair, the bible does teach us, "The righteous falls seven times and rises again." So when we fall, we do get up. The key in seeing Jesus exalted in our falling and failing is showing others how we were able to rise. In other words, anyone can fall. In fact, everyone does fall. But not everyone will get up. As we face major blows, supreme failures and devastating disappointments, Jesus is most glorified as he is put on display as the rescuer and redeemer for the shamed. You will be able to boast in Jesus because your failure will not define you since Jesus has bore all the shame. Get up. Your misstep or poor leadership is not what will shape your future because Jesus "orders the steps of a righteous man." You will rise.

PAIN

Another gateway into humility is pain. Honestly, if pain is one of the on-ramps for the superhighway of humility, most days I'd rather stay home. And yet for people my age (I'm forty), many of us have yet to truly experience real pain. Sure, I have had my share fair of scraped knees and black eyes, but real pain? Not yet.

My father, who is now in his eighties, was being treated recently for bone cancer. Up until his illness he was in relatively good health. He could walk, travel with his wife, and enjoy good food. His vitality was high. During his treatment, he was given a new chemotherapy drug that reacted badly with his own body chemistry. Within a week he was paralyzed from the waist down. In addition, he was in constant pain and forced to eat through a tube. My dad's life was full of pain. What I failed to mention was that my dad also did not have a personal relationship with Jesus Christ. He, along with my entire family, was Jewish. But while his body was in pain, his soul began to awaken to its need for real life. Of course that real life is only found in a relationship with God through His Son Jesus Christ. My dad cried out and was miraculously saved and is now a follower of Jesus Christ. The catalyst for my dad's conversion? Pain. Pain was a gift. It's a gift to you and to me as well.

Read the Psalmist as he ponders his own pain: "It was good that I was afflicted that I might learn your decrees." Even in my minor aches I have never said to my wife, "It's good that I am hurting." More often, my hurting leads to complaining, and my wife then says something like, "If you think you hurt now, keep complaining." Just kidding. Though it is true, we hate pain. It is never welcomed or seen as a gift. At best we see our sickness, disease, or frailty as an inconvenience. At worst, we begin to see God as someone who has abandoned us. We begin to say to ourselves, "If God really loved me, he wouldn't let me experience this kind of pain." But that idea of God just isn't true. In fact, the author of Hebrews says it this way, "Although He (Jesus) was a son, he learned obedience by what he suffered." In fact, when you read Isaiah 53, you find out that Jesus's suffering was planned by the Father.

> *But he was pierced for our transgressions, he was crushed for our iniquities; the punishment that brought us peace was on him, and by his wounds we are healed. ⁶ We all, like sheep, have gone astray, each of us has turned to our own way; and the Lord has laid on him the iniquity of us all. ⁷ He was oppressed and afflicted, yet he did not open his mouth; he was led like a lamb to the slaughter, and as a sheep before its shearers is silent, so he did not open his mouth. ⁸ By oppression and judgment he was taken away. Yet who of his generation protested? For he was cut off from the land of the living; for the transgression of my people he was punished. ⁹ He was assigned a grave with the wicked, and with the rich in his death, though he had done no violence, nor was any deceit in his mouth. ¹⁰ Yet it was the Lord's will to crush him and cause him to suffer, and though the Lord makes his life*

an offering for sin, he will see his offspring and prolong his days, and the will of the Lord will prosper in his hand.

Jesus—God's only son—suffered by the intentional, sovereign hand of God. Don't miss the point, though: Jesus' pain was for a purpose. While our pain has no Messianic properties to save or heal, our discomfort will always provide a path to get low and display Jesus as our ultimate worth. There are several ways you can leverage your pain for God's glory and your humility. Here are a few:

First, evaluate how your pain (physical or emotional) can be used to drive you to Christ and his comfort. John Piper, in his little book, *Don't Waste Your Cancer,* writes, "Satan's and God's designs in our cancer are not the same. Satan designs to destroy our love for Christ. God designs to deepen our love for Christ. Cancer does not win if we die. It wins if we fail to cherish Christ. God's design is to wean us off the breast of the world and feast us on the sufficiency of Christ. It is meant to help us say and feel, "I count everything as loss because of the surpassing worth of knowing Christ Jesus my Lord" (Philippians 3:8). While you may not be battling cancer, the principle is the same. Don't waste that pain through empty complaint and bitter conversation, but use it as a driving force to experience the Holy Spirit as the ultimate comforter.

I love pizza and ribs. When I'm feeling down, it's not uncommon for me to order a rack of ribs, a pound of Swedish fish candy, and eat my fill. They are my comfort foods. I eat and try to forget. Isn't it interesting that the Holy Spirit is called the Comforter (John 14:26)? He is the one we are meant to lean on and find comfort in. Unfortunately, when are you and me best comforted? In our pain and loss. Let your pain drive you to the comfort of God.

Second, begin to think and pray for others who are hurting. Have you ever thought that maybe your pain is for someone else?

The apostle Paul reminds us when he writes, "Blessed be the God and Father of our Lord Jesus Christ, the Father of mercies and God of all comfort, [4] who comforts us in all our affliction, so that we may be able to comfort those who are in any affliction, with the comfort with which we ourselves are comforted by God" (2 Corinthians 1:3–4). God is so intent on being made known, being exalted and being the treasure of every human heart, that he will use your pain and God's subsequent comfort as conduits for the sake of others. God desires that your friends and neighbors meet the comforter. Because we are self-centered people, sometimes God will use pain to stop us in our tracks to help us see the needs of those around us. Who are a few people in your life who are in pain that God may want you to comfort with the comfort given you?

Lastly, ask God to give you a greater burden for the eternal needs of others. If pain reminds us of anything, it is that this life is frail and comes to an end very quickly. Psalm 90:12 says, "Teach us to number our days that we may get a heart of wisdom." A heart of wisdom would be a heart that sees this life as short but eternity as unending. Plead with God that he would help you see past your own pain into the aches of other people's hearts. While not everyone is aware of their desperate need to be in relationship with Jesus, their hearts long for what they were made for. Isn't this what Solomon reminds us of when he said, "Also, he has put eternity into man's heart, yet so that he cannot find out what God has done from the beginning to the end" (Ecclesiastes 3:11).

PERSPECTIVE

My wife and I have been all around the world for missions. The last eighteen years have been an incredible gift to us as we have met with the church and church leaders in different contexts. Every time we get off a plane in a new country, we are ready for distinct smells, exotic foods, new languages, and of course, extreme poverty. It's not uncommon for teams we are part of to experience severe culture shock as they watch orphans begging in the streets or families drinking out of filthy wells. The guilt comes quickly. Inevitably, someone on the team will say, "I feel terrible. I own eighteen pairs of shoes and they own none! We Americans are so selfish!" Processing our emotions is critical in moments like these. We tell mission teams that it's not sinful to be an American but it is sinful to go back an unchanged American." You see, perspective should change everything! I believe as you and I pursue humility God will open our eyes to see what is most important in our lives.

Perspective is tricky, though. We never want to compare our lives to another. Comparison always leads to pride—either self-pity or self-righteousness. However, in moments where we have been removed from our context, clarity is often the result. Perspective is seeing the same things in a new way. For example, you may be living in a difficult marriage. The heat and romance leaked out years ago and you just wonder how God can be glorified in something so arduous. But then you read a book on marriage. Or maybe you have an encounter with God during your devotional time. All of a sudden you are able to see your spouse in a different way. She is no longer someone to be endured, but to be cherished. He isn't just someone you share a bed with, but someone God gave to you as a gift. Perspective has the potential to turn hopeless situations into great possibilities. And there is nothing that humbles us more than seeing God doing something that seems impossible.

While perspective is not something you can always manufacture, when it does happen, there are a couple ways you can leverage it for your good and God's glory.

First, begin to ask God where you need perspective. Every car has what is called blind spots. Blind spots are areas around the car that the driver cannot directly see while at the controls. Every person has blind spots, too. There are areas in your life that you just can't see while you are in control. Others can see them clearly, but you can't. The only way for you to even get a glimpse is for you to get a different vantage point. Ask God to help you step out from behind the wheel and take a look. Of course, pride will tell you that you don't need perspective, everyone else needs it! However, a different vantage point gives you a shot at seeing your greatest weakness (pride), and turning it into a great strength (dependence on God).

Secondly, ask some other people where you need perspective. Godly community is paramount in learning to get low. The key word here is "godly" community. Don't just ask any old dummy in your life. Sit down with a friend who loves Jesus deeply and loves you enough that he/she won't mind hurting your feelings for a minute. After all, the bible says, "Wounds from a friend can be trusted" (Proverbs 27:6). Ask the person to give you an honest assessment about your attitude. You could phrase it like, "I'd really like to cultivate a life of humility and other-centeredness, so what areas of my life have I made myself the hero?" or "Are there one or two places in my life that I have blind spots?" While it may be hard to hear their comments, receive them with gratitude. Your friend has been seeing these areas of deficit in your life for a long time and you're just seeing them for the first time. Your first instinct will be to defend yourself—don't do it. Simply thank them and then take them to the Lord in prayer.

PERSECUTION

If there is any area in the Christian experience that the American church lacks in, then it is none other than persecution. Not only do churches not talk about it, most Christians don't even have a context to understand it. Persecution, for many believers, falls into the same category as miracles—they know they exist, but they have never seen them. And because of the scarcity, there is almost no expectation for Christians to pay any price for following Christ. Persecution has been removed part and parcel from the American Christian culture. So much so, we are outraged to hear that Christians "rights" are being infringed upon. Schools are banning prayer. Kids are even being suspended for wearing Christian themed t-shirts. Yet Christians aren't praising God because they are able to identify with Christ's sufferings; instead, they lawyer up.

However, by God's design, persecution is a means in which the church is refined and humbled to trust God more than ever before. If a Christ-follower loses a promotion or a business is hindered because of his or her gospel witness, they are experiencing a measure of persecution. When a Christ-follower is being antagonized and his reputation suffers, he is experiencing a form of persecution. It is during those times of loss that the gospel response is to get low, see God as the greatest worth, and let God distribute justice by His wisdom.

Jesus tells a parable in Mark 4 about a man who was sowing seed. He tossed some seed on the sidewalk, other fell among the rocks, some fell among the thorns, and still some fell on good soil. For the life of them, the disciples couldn't figure out the meaning of this story. Jesus proceeds to explain that the seed represents the Word of God, and the place in which the seed falls represents a person's heart. Read Jesus' description of the seed that fell among thorns. "And others are the ones sown among thorns. They are those who hear the word, but the cares of the world and the deceitfulness of riches and the desires for other things enter in and choke the word, and it proves unfruitful." (vv. 18–19) Unfortunately, these verses paint a very accurate picture of many Christians in America. We are more interested in what this world can offer. We have bought into the dream of having it all. Life, we believe, is about us.

It would make sense then that persecution is a refining fire that removes "the cares of this world and the deceitfulness of riches" that will "choke the word." God will use everything at his disposal to get us low and dependent upon his mercy. It is no surprise when Paul reminds his disciple Timothy, "Indeed, all who desire to live a godly life in Christ Jesus will be persecuted" (2 Timothy 3:12). Are you experiencing any persecution or suffering for the sake of Christ? If not, is it because you have bought into the lie that says you can have it all and still follow Christ?

How can persecution be used to bring you low? Let me give you a few ways to leverage this truth:

First, pray for boldness in your walk with Christ. Often our desire to fit in with culture neuters our faith and keeps us from really living the life of boldness that Jesus desires. Ask the Lord to give you opportunity to open your mouth concerning the gospel. Listen to how the disciples prayed even as they were already experiencing persecution, "And now, Lord, look upon their threats and grant to your servants to continue to speak your word with all boldness" (Acts 4:29). Ironically, boldness will often beget boldness. The more you open your mouth about the grace of God, the more you will feel empowered to do so.

Secondly, look for ways to risk for the sake of the gospel. Don't look for persecution; look for ways to shine a light on the goodness of God. Feed the hungry, pray for the sick, share the good news of Jesus with your coworker. Do the work of Jesus, but be prepared and encouraged in Jesus' warning, "If the world hates you, keep in mind that it hated me first." (John 15:18)

Lastly, prepare yourself and your family for a measure of persecution. You're probably not reading this in the Sudan or in the heart of Afghanistan where you may actually lose your life for confessing Christ. But that's not to say you won't pay a price here in the US for following Jesus. Remind yourself that this world is not your home and you should not get too comfortable here. You are an alien in a foreign land and, rightly so, you may be treated like one.

CORRECTION

Solomon warns, "He who loves discipline loves knowledge; but he who hates correction is stupid" (Proverbs 12:1). If there is one universal thing we all dislike, it's correction. No one naturally responds well to being corrected. At best I can grin and bear it, and at worst, I bite back with all my teeth. Of course, a healthy dose of correction can lead to a posture of humility.

After being married to the same woman for nineteen years, I have discovered that I am usually wrong in our arguments. No false humility here—I'm a moron. I am very familiar with receiving gentle correction from her. Even though correction may come in a gentle way, it can still be incredibly painful to receive. However, after the sting and after I war against the feelings that I'm being attacked, I realize how loved I am to be corrected. In that moment I was brought low. As I repent, God exalts me to a place of right relationship.

This form of humility takes place when another person is loving enough to bring correction to a hard and rebellious heart. While correction never looks the same, it will always include a generous helping of gentleness (Galatians 6:1). It may happen over coffee and conversation and a gentle nudge is given. Correction may have a bolder flavor as someone meets you at your home because they want to have a real heart-to-heart with you over your abusive attitude at work. It can happen in private. It can even happen publicly if your pride-filled offense is done in public (Galatians 2:11–14). The point is that God has designed correction to bring us to a place of submission to other people. In fact, Paul commands the Romans to submit to an unjust authority (Romans 13:1–2) because as we submit in difficult circumstances, it readies our heart to submit to the Lord.

How do you respond to correction? Do you regularly argue or justify your behavior when someone lovingly corrects you? Let me give a few ways you can take advantage of these painful moments of correction for your humility:

First, just take it. Chances are everyone knows about your brokenness and frailty except you. So don't argue or put up a fight. Don't bow up on the other person and say, "Oh, yeah? Well, you're no peach either!" Just take it. Endure it knowing that your pride has been exposed and you now have the option to repent and walk in freedom. And tell the person that you are grateful for their courage to correct you.

Secondly, get a second opinion. If this counsel seems oddly familiar, it should. In the same way that you will likely visit multiple doctors so they can look at that weird rash you have, you should also meet with several close friends to ask their opinions concerning your dark heart and behavior. These second opinions are not so you can disprove what another person has observed. These alternate sources will only give you greater clarity on an area of your life that you have been blind to for years. For example, you go to meet Friend A and she tells you that she has watched you consistently tell lies by exaggerating and stretching the truth. You then meet with Friend B and ask her if he has seen that same kind of behavior and what it looks like. Don't meet with Friend B and say, "Dang, I didn't realize how stupid Friend A is. What a nut job!" Find out what your friends already know about you—you're broken, self-centered, and full of pride. But you don't have to stay that way.

Third, repent well. Repentance is the bread and butter of our faith in Jesus Christ. The moment we remove repentance from the church is the moment we cease being the church. Jesus never asks us to simply change our behavior, he asks us to surrender our hearts, desires, and agenda to him. Behavior change—at least long-term behavior change—occurs as we repent and surrender our hearts to God. Listen to the observations of your gospel community, take the correction, and then repent. Turn away from your sin and pursue making Jesus the treasure of your words, work, and behavior. Repenting well often means repenting *often*. Don't buy into the fast food idea of growth. Your sanctification will happen on the long road of obedience and continual times of repentance.

PURSUIT

The last doorway into humility should have been the first, but no one starts here. As we've seen, God will use everything in His arsenal for the sake of a meek heart. While persecution and failure certainly is a good place to begin, a single-minded pursuit of humility will get us where we need to be a lot faster. The apostle Peter gives us this instruction: "Humble yourselves, therefore, under the mighty hand of God so that at the proper time he may exalt you…" (1 Peter 5:6). If you want to be Christlike, humble *yourself*. Don't wait to be humbled. Quit looking over your shoulder thinking at any moment God has caught up with your proud heart. Humble yourself first. Get low now. Stop thinking you have all, or any, of the answers. Stop coaching yourself into thinking that you have to make something happen.

There is a beautiful promise for those of us who follow through with the command of humbling ourselves— *"He may exalt you."* What does it mean that God may exalt you? It simply means that you will be given a greater platform to display the immeasurable worth and value of Jesus Christ. As you slowly dismantle your own platform that was for your glory, God builds a foundation for you so that He can be made much of in your life. You are exalted so that He may be exalted.

Jesus says in Matthew 6:33, *"But seek first the kingdom of God and then all these things will be added to you."* The same principle is at work here as in 1 Peter 5. If you will seek the Kingdom of God first, then all that you need will be given to you. As you humble yourself, the very thing you wanted in the first place will actually happen—you will be exalted. But this exaltation will look very different from the world's exaltation. God will raise you up, but it will no longer be about you. You will constantly deflect the honor. God will lift you up just so you can lift him up even higher. True humility always begets greater worship.

It's easy to be humbled and made to be low. But how do we humble ourselves? What does it really look like? In the next chapter we'll begin to talk through very practical, everyday ways.

CHAPTER 5

When the Hero Dies

I like clean, feel-good movie endings. If I pay $13 dollars for a movie experience, I want the boy to get the girl, the spy to kill the villain, and the prisoner to go free. I want the happy ending. When I don't get it, I get mad. However, happy endings aren't always happy for everyone. Sometimes the hero dies. This is certainly true in the greatest story of humility—Jesus dies. Not only does he die, he lays down his life. He becomes low so that we can be exalted.

Sometimes heroes die.

If the last chapter contained ways God creates opportunities for you to be humbled, this next chapter is about ways you create opportunities to humble yourself. I want to be careful here because I don't want to boil humility down to a list. Lists are dangerous because they can easily cultivate a performance mentality. However, sometimes a list is just what we need. Not always. But sometimes I just need to be told where to go, what to do, what to say, how to say it, and when to keep my mouth shut. So if you're asking, "How can I [be] more humble?" On the one hand I want to say, "Just do these 8 things, dummy. Don't overthink this!" But on the other hand we need to know what is the substance behind the list. That is, is there a difference between behaving with humility and actually having a heart of humility?

Can we get humble by acting humble?

I have wrestled through this idea for several years now and keep hearing Forest Gump whisper in my ear, "Stupid is as stupid does." So, according to his theology, humility is as humility does. Sounds right. But is it right? It's complicated. God seems to constantly juxtapose our behavior against our heart and remind us that our behavior is not what defines our humility. Then God gives us all these commands on how to humble ourselves. Do you see why this is a bit complex? For example, in Isaiah 58 God is chastising the way that Judah is fasting. He's like, "I told you to fast. I told you to humble yourself. But HOW you're doing it is all wrong."

> *Why have we fasted, and you see it not? Why have we humbled ourselves, and you take no knowledge of it?' Behold, in the day of your fast you seek your own pleasure, and oppress all your workers. ⁴ Behold, you fast only to quarrel and to fight and to hit with a wicked fist. Fasting like yours this day will not make your voice to be heard on high. ⁵ Is such the fast that I choose, a day for a person to humble himself?* (Isaiah 58:3-5)

There are very few behaviors more conducive in our pursuit of humility than fasting. And yet in this passage God seems to say, "Quit fasting! Don't try to play games with me. I know you look humble, but your heart is still full of pride, full of anger, full of ambition, full of, well, you!" Apparently, humble behavior does not equal humility. And yet at the same exact time, humility is defined by how we lay down our rights, forgive our enemies, and submit our agendas to the Lord. Sounds like behavior to me.

This is where I have landed thus far in my pursuit of getting low and seeing Jesus lifted high in my life. There are some parts of our character development, as Jesus followers, that simply come easier to us than other areas. It's all grace, but there are some things in our hearts that we just have to fight for. For example, learning that God provides for every need in your life may have come fairly easy to you because of your background. You grew up with missionary parents in the middle of war-torn Somalia and all you ever knew was that God supernaturally provided for your family.

In contrast, you may not be a very forgiving person. Perhaps your roommate in college deeply wounded you and you're not sure you can ever forgive her. You think your life will never be the same because of her deception. For you, trust in provision comes easy and yet forgiveness is something you'll have to fight for. In the same way, humility is something we all must wrestle for and at the same time receive as a gift from God. Becoming the person God intended you to be is a work of grace, but it also means you have to put that grace to work.

Let me illustrate it this way: imagine you are a lumberjack. You have one of those massive axes that can really do damage to a tree. On Monday you go to work and the only trees you have to cut down are pine trees just 4 inches in diameter. This job will only take you three to four swings of your ax per tree. But on Tuesday you are tasked with chopping down the largest sequoia in the world. It's called General Sherman, located in the Sequoia National Park in Tulare County, California. Its diameter is 36.5 feet wide. Behemoth is an understatement. It's going to take you more than a few swings to knock this thing over. In fact, you look at that massive tree and think to yourself, *Is this even possible?* But you sharpen your ax and you go to work and, 8,000 swings later, that tree is falling to the ground. In the same way, there are some parts of the disciple's life that comes easy. A few swings and the tree of patience is firmly established in your character. A few more swings and joy is woven into your circumstances. But there are other parts of your spiritual life that require real, sustained work. Hear me: I'm not saying void of grace. I'm saying empowered to work, by grace. Paul answers it this way:

> *"But by the grace of God I am what I am, and his grace toward me was not in vain. On the contrary, I worked harder than any of them, though it was not I, but the grace of God that is with me."* (1 Corinthians 15:10)

Like Paul, we are empowered by the Holy Spirit and filled with the grace of God, so we might labor towards humility. We fight for it. We do battle against our flesh, our mouth, our desires and our ambition and pursue what will make us most Christlike. Now don't forget, you are already Christlike. Because of Jesus' death, burial, resurrection, and now abiding presence in your life, God sees you as fully righteous, holy, and humble. That is what you are! So our actions and behavior now place our lives congruent with who we already are spiritually.

FIGHTCLUB

A few years ago our church had to navigate a very difficult season—one of the leaders in our church confessed to a moral failure. Our church was devastated. This man who, for years, had led prayer meetings, pastored the hurting, and had given oversight to our church family had turned out to be, well, someone else. After weeks of difficult conversations with family members and close friends, we discovered some very strange behavior leading up to this spiritual fracture. Are you ready for this? The strange behavior was that this guy read his bible every day. Yep. Every day. A proverb, three Psalms, and a gospel reading were part of his regular spiritual diet. He regularly shared his faith at work. He gave generously to missions and to the work of the gospel. And, to boot, the mission field wasn't something foreign to him. He went for weeks at a time and lived in foreign cultures to bring the gospel to unreached peoples. This guy was the model Christian until his sin caught up with him.

Several folks in our church asked the obvious question: "How could someone who behaves this way become a leader in our church?" The answer: he drifted. Not all at once. But over time he drifted. This man had zero intention of shipwrecking this season of his life. His outward spiritual behavior was stellar all the while he had stopped fighting for his heart.

FIGHTING ~~FOR~~ YOUR RIGHTS

If we're fighting for our hearts, forget fighting fair. There is no fair when it comes to your life. Gouge the eyes, hit the crotch, and pull the hair. Your flesh and certainly the adversary of your soul is ruthless and you and I must make war. Of course our weapons are not of this world, but they are weapons of warfare (2 Corinthians 10:4–5). We must take aim at one of the most guarded and cherished strongholds: our rights.

> *We hold these truths to be sacred and undeniable; that all men are created equal and independent, that from that equal creation they **derive rights inherent and inalienable**, among which are the preservation of life, and liberty, and the pursuit of happiness.*

The Declaration of Independence underscores for us the undeniable right among Americans to be happy. We believe that right trumps everyone and everything else around us. A person, organization, even God, does not have the right to infringe on my personal liberty. Cue the fireworks and Lee Greenwood's *God Bless the USA*! Here's the rub , though: as Americans we do have rights. We are entitled to certain benefits of belonging to this country. But we are not only citizens of the United States. We are citizens and members of another kingdom. And this Kingdom operates with a different set of rules, standards, and expectations. As a Kingdom of God citizen, we no longer are entitled to anything but joyful submission to God and the betterment of people around us. Our inherent and inalienable right to do and be and pursue anything we want has now been replaced by the explicit love and will of our King Jesus. Pursuit of our best has been replaced by what is best for the name of Jesus Christ.

STEAK AND MALBEC

Laying down our rights, whatever they may be, are part and parcel in the life of a disciple. A person who demands her agenda but also confesses the Lordship of Jesus doesn't yet understand where her allegiance lies. A man who demands fairness in this world is a man who doesn't yet understand that we may be the most hated and reviled of all people because of our identification with the cross.

The apostle Paul had to remind the Corinthian church of this truth again and again. For example, in 1 Corinthians 8, it appears that Paul is responding to a weird cultural question from these young disciples, "Can we get demon-possessed by eating meat that was sacrificed in a pagan temple?" Paul's answer: "Don't be stupid." OK, that's the Jon Quitt translation. But these believers were worried because they knew that by worshipping a pagan god, demons were being worshipped. So the progression goes, if that meat is sacrificed to a demon, perhaps that meat is demon-possessed. And if a person eats that meat, they will be demon-possessed as well. I see the logic. Paul's response? "If you can get a T-bone at a discount by shopping at Dagon's Meat Market, go for it!" He actually says, *Food will not commend us to God. We are no worse off if we do not eat, and no better off if we do* (v. 8). In other words, "You have the right to eat that meat offered to idols." But notice the following instructions,

⁹ But take care that this right of yours does not somehow become a stumbling block to the weak. ¹⁰ For if anyone sees you who have knowledge eating in an idol's temple, will he not be encouraged, if his conscience is weak, to eat food offered to idols? ¹¹ And so by your knowledge this weak person is destroyed, the brother for whom Christ died. ¹² Thus, sinning against your brothers and wounding their conscience when it is weak, you sin against Christ. ¹³ Therefore, if food makes my brother stumble, I will never eat meat, lest I make my brother stumble.

If our rights get in the way of the gospel, we are to lay them down joyfully. If a brother's faith and conscience is weak and yet you demand your right and liberty in spite of your brother, Paul contends that the weaker man's faith may be destroyed. Paul continues this line of thought two chapters later,

"All things are lawful," but not all things are helpful. "All things are lawful," but not all things build up. ²⁴ Let no one seek his own good, but the good of his neighbor. ²⁵ Eat whatever is sold in the meat market without raising any question on the ground of conscience. ²⁶ For "the earth is the Lord's, and the fullness thereof."

Paul is making a pretty big theological statement here. Because Jesus has fulfilled all the demands of the law, there is nothing that can affect our standing with God. However, just because "all things are permissible" for us does not mean "all things are helpful" for our younger brothers or sisters.

²⁷ If one of the unbelievers invites you to dinner and you are disposed to go, eat whatever is set before you without raising any question on the ground of conscience. ²⁸ But if someone says to you, "This has been offered in sacrifice," then do not eat it, for the sake of the one who informed you, and for the sake of conscience— [29] I do not mean your conscience, but his. For why should my liberty be determined by someone else's conscience? [30] If I partake with thankfulness, why am I denounced because of that for which I give thanks? [31] So, whether you eat or drink, or whatever you do, do all to the glory of God.

Let me try to bring this home. I drink wine. My wife and I often enjoy a nice bottle of Malbec with dinner. It is not unusual for us to drink a glass, two or three times a week. We have friends who also enjoy wine as well. However, I pastor a church filled with people in recovery and are broken because of addiction. Because my calling is to shepherd people like this and to lead them to places of wholeness, I regularly lay down my right to drink wine. A couple of nights a week Amy and I will entertain guests in our home. However, we never pull out the wine. We don't talk about our hobby of trying new wines and pairing them with different kinds of meat. We choose to lay down our rights of drinking wine. We remind ourselves, "If this wine will make this brother stumble, I will not drink this wine."

And yet I have met other believers who just can't embrace this idea. They say things like, "This is my right! All things are permissible! If people have a problem with my freedom in the Lord, that's their problem!" Unfortunately for these believers, they don't yet understand that following Christ means checking our rights at the door. We are bond-servants of Christ and we serve him, not only so He will be honored but so that brothers or sisters do not stumble.

One more example will hopefully nail down this idea. We live in a culture and time when some women wear clothing that is, well, revealing. Modesty now moves along a varying spectrum, beginning with a nun's habit and ending with two toiler paper squares getting fashioned together with dental floss. Some women who are disciples of Jesus have lost sight of others' frailty and will wear anything that draws attention to their body. Before you get mad at me, I get it! I really do. Some women are really proud of their body and wear clothing to show off the hard work done at the gym. Unfortunately, this can also be a massive blind spot for women. Many women are not aware of the frailty of a man's heart. In fact, most men I know desire to be faithful in action and thought to God and their wives. Purity for men is a big deal. I've heard of godly men asking women they are in community with a mind to think about what they wear because it impacts the thought-life of those around them. The responses have varied from "Thank you, I will pray about that," to, "Shut your pie hole you judgmental jerk!" I'm not joking.

These conversations are necessary in the community of Jesus. Most are truly unaware that their lives are not their own anymore. Our lives and bodies and preferences now belong to Jesus. This is not to say men and women aren't people with feelings and opinions and deep-rooted beliefs. I'm just saying that if our rights are not regularly submitted to Jesus, His supremacy is undermined and our desire for people's best is diminished.

I love the illustration I read from Pastor Ray Ortland. It goes like this: you and I in the recess of our hearts have a boardroom. This boardroom looks like any other boardroom. It has a big mahogany table with twelve wingback chairs around it and a white erase board in the corner. The chairs belong to your board members. The members of your board are the future you, the past you, the child you, the procrastinator you, and so on. Every time there is a decision to be made, your board votes and then you make a choice. However, when you come to faith in Christ and the Holy Spirit indwells you, he sits down at your big mahogany table and he fires your entire board. He's not interested in votes. He doesn't care about the tally. God is now in charge and calling the shots of your life.

GOD AND GOVERNMENT

Laying down our rights is not something that comes naturally. It's not like being left-handed or having rhythm. You don't just have it. Getting low and submitting our desires to God for the sake of others takes persistence and diligence. Thankfully, God has provided several avenues for you and me as we learn to submit ourselves and our rights.

"Let every person be subject to the governing authorities. For there is no authority except from God, and those that exist have been instituted by God. ² Therefore whoever resists the authorities resists what God has appointed, and those who resist will incur judgment." (Romans 13:1-2)

The progression of this text flows like this: God created the government. Submit to the government. If you choose not to submit, then you're choosing not to submit to the Lord. And if you rebel against the Lord, judgment is coming.

These are fairly stern words especially for those who dislike or even disagree with our government and current legislation. Certainly Paul can't be saying we have to endorse every wicked, unjust, or immoral practice the government manages. Of course not! (Acts 5:27–28) If he's not saying that, then what is he saying? At the heart of these commands is this: real submission is tested in disagreeable situations. If you love your authority, then it takes no real energy to submit to that authority. But when you feel pushed around, slighted, and even persecuted by your authority, all of a sudden you feel justified in defending your own rights.

Just because you and I don't like the authority doesn't mean we have the biblical right to disobey that authority—because that authority was placed there by God.

For example, you may have an unjust and unfair boss that you work for. She looks for ways to make your life difficult. There have even been moments where she even publicly humiliated you in front of your coworkers. She may be the devil, or so you think. Have you thought, perhaps, that God placed her in your life for you to learn humility? Maybe God handpicked your boss, in his mysterious providence, to help you learn to get low. And ironically, every time you kick against your boss, guess what? You kick against God.

Read Peter's version of this same command.

"Be subject for the Lord's sake to every human institution, whether it be to the emperor as supreme, [14] or to governors as sent by him to punish those who do evil and to praise those who do good. [15] For this is the will of God, that by doing good you should put to silence the ignorance of foolish people. [16] Live as people who are free, not using your freedom as a cover-up for evil, but living as servants of God." (1 Peter 2:13–16)

I can't imagine anyone could read this and ask, "I wonder if God wants me to submit to authorities?" What a person might ask, though, is: why would God want me to submit to _all_ authorities? God raises up governments, companies, bosses, parents, and pastors to be tools in His hand so we might experience the gift of submission and humility. Of course, it's our choice whether we choose to get low and learn how to conform our lives to Jesus' image.

I find that most people, really, really admire Jesus. But most people don't really want to be like Jesus. They love that Jesus washed his disciples' feet, but they certainly don't want to live lives of service. Unfortunately, God is so intent on you and me learning godly submission that even in difficult circumstances, he will continue to give us ample opportunities. Meaning: every time you quit a job because your boss is unjust or exit a ministry position because you're not being promoted, what you will find is that God will continue to put you in the same situation until you learn to get low. Remember, God's primary interest is not promoting you, but conforming you to the image of His Son.

OBEYING JESUS AND THE BIBLE

If governing authorities is the blunt force tool of the Holy Spirit to conform us to Jesus' image and help us fight for humility, then obedience to simple truths of the scripture is the scalpel. There is not one man or woman that I admire as a humble follower of Jesus that is not serious about obeying God and His Word. I know this seems elementary. It is. But I can't tell you how many conversations I've had with people who are always looking for the loophole and the exception to what the bible commands. "I know the bible says this, but does that really apply to this situation?" "I understand what this verse says, but surely God understands my heart for doing it my way."

Please understand the goal isn't to obey the scriptures. The goal is to look like Jesus, live like Jesus, and respond like Jesus. The scriptures are never an end in themselves. Even Jesus reminded the Pharisees of this in John 9. *"You search the Scriptures because you think that in them you have eternal life;* (v. 39) But Jesus did continually point people to the scriptures. *"And it is they that bear witness about me, ⁴⁰ yet you refuse to come to me that you may have life."* (v. 39)

Jesus obeyed the scriptures and fulfilled all the demands of the law, because he knew we were unable to on our own. He took the weight of the law so we could enjoy the benefits of the law. Meaning, we don't obey the scriptures because in doing so Jesus will accept us. We obey the scriptures because we have already been accepted by Jesus. The commands of the scriptures are now gifts to those of us who long to know Jesus deeply and to be shaped into His image.

Several challenges are in play for those who long to obey the scriptures. First, you will need to become acquainted with the Scriptures. I'm not going to belabor this idea, but begin to read your bible everyday. Even David said, *"Oh how I love your law! It is my meditation all the day."* (Psalm 119:97) Learning to get low, humbling yourself to God's plan is dependent on you and me knowing God's plan and purpose. There's just not much of an excuse for saying, "I didn't know the Bible said that!" Download an app, read it on your tablet, buy a robust devotional. Whatever. Begin to find out what God says and obey it—even if you don't understand it. Your obedience is not contingent on your understanding. Even if obeying goes against every grain of your being, obey it. Even if no one else around you is obeying, obey it.

Obedience is an enormous doorway to the realm of humility. Our obedience to God's commands reveals the affections of our heart toward Him. Jesus said it this way in John 14, *"If you love me, you will keep my commandments."* As we learn to trust Jesus, our desire and willingness to obey grow as well. What I hear fairly often from people is, "Jon, this sounds like legalism. We are set free from obeying the law!" My response is always the same, "Legalism is obeying rules so that a person will be accepted by God." Because we are already accepted by God through the finished work of Jesus Christ, our motives for obeying are different. We long to obey because we know his commands are for our best. Obedience is not legalism. Obedience is a result of love that leads to humility.

Several of the apostles would often refer to themselves as bondservants of Christ (James 1:1, 2 Peter 1:1, Romans 1:1). A bondservant is someone who was once free who now willingly lays down his rights for a master. A bondservant is a willing slave. Our lives are to be lived in joyful submission to ALL of our master's commands. And yet so often we are selective on how and what we will obey.

For example, stealing is a sin. Even a first grader in Sunday school knows that one. But what is stealing really? Sure, don't grab your neighbor's 80-inch TV and pawn it. That's stealing and it's wrong! You would never do that, I'm sure. But what about downloading music from the Internet that you didn't purchase? Still stealing? This is where the fancy footwork of bad theology comes in. I'll hear, "Well, it's not really stealing, 'cause it's not hurting anyone. The music is just out in space and I'm reaching out and getting it." Or suppose you buy a single license for a computer program. You are only permitted with this license to put it on a single computer. But you decide to load it on a second computer as well and you say, "What's the harm? They will never know and it's not like they need the money!" You may label this "complex ethics," but Jesus calls it stealing.

You will never regret obeying in the secret places. Humility is born in moments of quiet submission as you choose to obey in small areas of your life. Obedience is a key component for your humility. You may have many small reasons not to obey, but there is one supremely important reason *to* obey. We obey because Jesus is our treasure and there is nothing else worth giving our affection and obedience to.

Living in the deep south of awkward and fractured evangelicalism, people often think, "I don't really have to obey, because Jesus *has to* forgive me. That's what He does!" While Jesus has paid the penalty of our sin on the cross, he has also, through the power of the Holy Spirit, given us the power over our sin. That means we no longer have to sin. We have a choice. Is Jesus glorified in forgiving us? Of course! But he is glorified to a greater degree when we depend on his power to say no to sin. It is in saying no to sin and yes to Jesus in which we display his worth and ability to satisfy us in every moment.

When disobedience becomes the norm, this is when we realize we are treasuring something more than Jesus. We know Jesus will forgive us because he is a loving Father. But the moment we demand that he must forgive is the moment we forget our place in this relationship. He is the Father and we are the children. He is Master and we are servants. He is Savior and we are sinners. Our place is as recipient, not as generous benefactor. You and I fight for humility as we know our place as son, daughter, servant, and recipient of grace.

FORGIVENESS

Forgiving those who have hurt us is a decisive blow in our fight for humility. Forgiveness sets us free from the demand of personal justice. Jesus reminds us, *"And will not God bring about justice for his chosen ones..."* (Luke 18:7). Our role is not to pursue justice, but to pursue God, who will dole out justice on our behalf. The knowledge that God, according to his righteousness, will set things right on our behalf, should give us great comfort—we no longer have to be in control! Forgiveness also sets us free from the need to be right. Having to be right is just another trap that looks holy, but is actually set for us by the devil. Our need to be right and the recognition of being right sets us up in opposition to the finished work of Jesus Christ. Our right-ness is only found in the righteousness of Christ. The moment our lives become a justification for withholding grace or forgiveness is the moment we have forgotten our identity as grace-receivers and beneficiaries of forgiveness.

There is a theological idea behind forgiveness that is often helpful for those of us who find ourselves in need of forgiveness or the need to forgive others. When a person sins, that sin is against God. I know this isn't rocket science. But follow me here. When a person lies to you, betrays your trust, or gossips about you, they have sinned against you—but they have first sinned against the Lord. Their failure to submit their tongue or actions to Jesus has created collateral damage to your soul, but ultimately they have first committed treason against the Creator. The reason this truth is so important is because of this: Jesus offers forgiveness to them. Because of Jesus' beautiful work on the cross, any person who repents and joyfully submits their lives to Christ will be forgiven. In fact, Jesus has gone to great lengths to provide forgiveness to people who do not even believe they need forgiveness. Jesus has pursued reconciliation with people who continue to spit in his face, revile against his character, and use his name as an expletive. Jesus continues to offer forgiveness to people who really don't deserve forgiveness.

Isn't that the issue? The reason we withhold forgiveness for so long is because we're waiting for those people who have hurt us to deserve our forgiveness. I'll let you in on a secret: they will never deserve it, because neither will you. Forgiveness is a gift—free, meritless, and it can never be paid back. The reason forgiveness is such a big deal is because true forgiveness only comes from God. The demand for justice has been paid in full by Jesus. Not only is Jesus the judge, but he is also the justifier. God must punish sin and so Jesus takes the full punishment of our sin on the cross. The result is forgiveness and freedom for those who place their trust in Christ.

I know women who have been raped by their father and I've seen the forgiveness of God over their life empower them to forgive their fathers. I've witnessed children forgive a parent ravaged by addiction. I've watched women forgive themselves after years of self-hatred because of an abortion. Forgiveness of others is only born out of an experience with the forgiveness of God.

A failure to forgive will mean a constant replay of the betrayal and pain in the movie theatre of your mind. What is meant to hold others captive by the withholding of your forgiveness is only holding you captive by your hurt. In addition, forgiveness is constantly keeping the attention on you. That's called pride. It's no wonder we're often reminded to *"set our eyes on Jesus, the author and perfector of our faith"* (Hebrews 12:2). Keeping our energy on ourselves is exhausting, and the only way to be set free from this kind of spiritual fatigue is forgiveness. And that forgiveness leads to a beautiful, gentle submission to a loving Father.

COMMUNITY AND DISCIPLESHIP

Up until now we've talked through ways to get in the fight for humility, but let me end with how to actually stay in the fight. Learn to walk deeply *with* other people. What does that mean, you ask? Well, it's not just joining a Sunday School class or getting in a small group at your church, though that will be helpful. What I mean is getting in a consistent, intentional discipleship relationship with someone who is several years ahead of you, someone who has walked with God in deep places of obedience and faith. This person will often have the aroma of humility. You will often find them behind the scenes praying, setting chairs up at church, caring for the marginalized, sending notes of encouragement to other leaders and generally pouring out their lives for no other reason than it gives Jesus the most glory. Having these kinds of people in your life means you are giving them real room to speak life, correction, and needed encouragement into your marriage, vocation, sexuality, and walk with Jesus. Because our lives are built around self-sufficiency, this will easily be the hardest, but most effective, way to fight and stay in the fight for humility with the Lord.

Submission to another person is an obvious model found in the scriptures. Aaron had Moses. Elisha had Elijah. Samuel had Eli. Peter, James, and John had Jesus. Timothy had Paul. Who do you have? Don't say your pastor. Just because he preaches the bible and faithfully challenges you to lay down rights does not mean he is actually involved in your life. Do you have a person whom you have given explicit permission to call you on your crap? Is there a woman who can stop you in your tracks when you start talking trash about your husband? Is there a man who can say to you with all his might, "Stop lying to me!"

Years ago I was just out of college and I landed my first ministry job. It was at a fairly large church and, while I was given a legitimate title, I was basically a glorified intern. I was perfectly happy with whatever they would give me because I knew I was there to learn. My direct report was to a man who was mentoring me and had enormous faith that I would do great things for the Lord. About a year into my role, I was given a fairly large project. I had performed well up to this point and my boss/mentor felt like it was time for me to stretch a bit. I was thrilled for the challenge. However, I realized fairly soon that I was in over my head. The administrative expectations combined with the relational component had me drowning. Instead of owning up to my inadequacies, I dug in deeper and tried to make something happen. Several weeks later I skated to the finish line, got the project done, but not without hurting several people in our church. I was hoping my failure would not find its way to my boss. A week later I was called into his office and he sat me down. He asked, "What happened here?" I himmed and hawed and tried to pass the blame. Somewhere in the middle of my excuses my mentor looked at me and said, "Don't do that. Don't pass the blame. You're going to be doing this job for a long time. Own your junk and move forward. Otherwise you'll be blaming people your whole life!" I took a deep breath, looked him in the eye, and confessed that I had dropped the ball about eighteen times.

That conversation was a defining mark for me. What my mentor did for me was speak directly into my life. His words impacted the direction and, perhaps, even the duration of my ministry. His words hurt, but they were medicine that I needed. Every disciple of Jesus needs someone who has that kind of permission to kick us in the gut with the truth of the gospel.

Since isolation breeds arrogance, it is of paramount importance that we stay connected to life-giving people. If you and I never have someone who will hold our feet to the fire and remind us that we are not God's gift to anyone, but simple servants to our family and gospel community, then true humility will elude us. It is incredibly healthy to have one or two people in our life who have total access and can just call us on our junk. They are the ones reminding you to keep your mouth shut, stop making excuses, keep obeying in your marriage, even when it hurts and a hundred more things. In short, they are keeping you from making yourself the hero.

Do you remember in Matthew 16 when Jesus was telling his disciples that he had to go to Jerusalem, be abused, forsaken, and ultimately die on a cross for mankind? Peter, one of Jesus' main disciples, takes Jesus aside because obviously Jesus doesn't understand how establishing a kingdom works. Peter says, *"Far be it from you, Lord! This shall never happen to you."* (v. 22) Peter was rebuking Jesus and telling him not to go to the cross. This was about as anti-mission as he could get. Now Jesus lets him have it: *"Get behind me, Satan! You are a hindrance to me. For you are not setting your mind on the things of God, but on the things of man!"* (v. 23) Jesus' relationship with Peter had so much depth that he could say something that would injure his heart, but would save his soul.

Thankfully I've never had anyone call me the devil, though some have come close. I do have a few people who have spoken such painful and yet helpful things into my soul that if they were not spoken, I may have shipwrecked my faith. Each of us requires that kind of community in our lives. Without these men and women, you and I will always become the hero, remain the hero, and die the hero in our own story. What you may never hear, however, is that dying the hero always means dying alone. A life of arrogance and pride will always keep people at arms length, lest they find out about the real you. Letting someone in, giving them permission to speak the gospel over your life, is truly fighting for your life and humility.

Of course this journey of deep gospel relationships will often take years to cultivate. Finding these people will take a bit of work, and cultivating a rhythm with your new mentor/disciple/friend will also take time. So while you are learning to submit to some older men or women in your life, it is also important for you to find a few people you are also cultivating by the power of the gospel. These are men and women you are helping learn what a joyfully submitted life looks like. While this idea may seem foreign to you, it's only because you and I have been brainwashed into thinking disciple-making is for the professionals. If you are a Jesus follower, filled with the Holy Spirit and working out your faith with fear and trembling, then you are the professional. Look around, see who God has brought into your life and ask them to coffee. Tell them you'd like to help them in their journey with God because someone has and is helping you. This is what Jesus people do! Don't overthink it. Do what you know, with who you know.

I have met with literally dozens of men over the course of the last twenty years. I usually meet early in the morning. We study a few verses together, we pray together, I ask them probing questions about their purity, dating, marriages, finances, and anything that is relevant. Sometimes a man will be caught off guard and tell me it's none of my business. I usually give them the short version of what you've just read and tell them I don't want to see them try to be a hero, 'cause they're not heroes. That's why they need someone who will help keep their life anchored to the person of Jesus Christ. Many of these men have gone on and entered vocational ministry. Most of them are faithfully serving their local churches, wives, and children and living lives with the aroma of satisfaction in the Lord. These men have learned to understand that they no longer have to make a name for themselves.

CHAPTER 6

What Now?

On our first date, I brought Amy a single flower. She loved it. I was an idealistic twenty-year-old who wanted to WOW this girl. Picking her up on the second date, I presented another flower. She smiled and gave me a kiss. I liked where this was going. This pattern continued for several months of our young relationship. It was beautiful and romantic. But, after a couple of months into our courtship, I began to feel the pressure. I thought to myself, *What will happen if I don't bring a flower? Will she still be into me?* So the flowers continued. Granted, my budget was limited, so the flowers were usually from the local grocery store. I'd grab whatever was under 99 cents. After all, it didn't really matter where the flowers came from, as long as she got one. Everything changed one afternoon—I had taken a nap and had overslept. I was now late for our date and I had to drive across town to pick her up. As I was pulling out of my apartment complex, I realized I didn't have the time or the money to get a flower. I was panicking. Driving, I noticed a local cemetery. Apparently someone very important had passed away because there were hundreds of fresh flowers on a freshly dug gravesite. I stopped my car. I psyched myself up and walked over to the casket, acted like a mourning friend, grabbed a rose, and nervously made my way back to the getaway car. That night, Amy loved her rose.

Now, before you judge me, before you cite some city statute to me, I already know! I am terribly embarrassed by my behavior. After all, I'm the only person I know who has committed a theft at a funeral. However, one nugget of truth has always come to the surface out of that story—I may have gotten the flower, but someone had to die for me to get it. This is the opposite of where we want to live. For you to get what you really want (humility), it means *you have to die*. You die to your wants, agendas, desires, and applause. And in doing so, you get the very thing your heart actually longs for.

Let me offer some final thoughts here on what it means, over the long-haul, to pursue a life lived for the glory of God and in pursuit of humility.

REPENT OFTEN

Let's hit the release valve for a second. Humility—you won't get this right. Nobody hits homeruns in humility. Base hits—that's all we do. So the pressure should be off, right? You don't have to be awesome. Simply put, submit your heart and life to the Lord everyday. The reason daily submission is so important is because you will blow it, often in big ways. You will, without even thinking, insert a quick anecdote into a conversation that makes you look a little smarter and more informed. The other person probably won't even notice, but you will. In fact, this happened even this morning to me. I lead a small group bible study for men on Thursday mornings at Dunkin Donuts. During our discussion, one of the men mentioned that he was reading a book that was written during the Holocaust. The book is fairly obscure, but what these men did not know is that I had read that same book fairly recently. So as this man is pouring out his heart and using a story from the book to reinforce his thought, I jump in with a quote out of the same book. Right after the words escaped my lips, I wanted to crawl inside myself. Why did I feel it was necessary to reveal I had read that book? Because I wanted the men to know I had read the book. I wanted them to respect how educated I was. I was, unashamedly, pursuing their approval. The men continued to talk amidst the doughnuts, but I was quietly repenting to the Lord, *I don't want to do that anymore.*

The more we become aware of our tendency to pursue admiration of people, the more we should lay that desire down before the Lord. Laying down our pride can and should be super practical. Look at the places of your life where you tend to make much of yourself, talk often of your accomplishments, or simply offer an uninvited opinion. Evaluate whether or not you tend to insert yourself into other people's worlds. I'm not talking about you tweeting your latest conquest in leading eighteen atheists to the Lord, though that could certainly qualify as a boast. It could include you simply posting your opinion on parenting, blogging your wise evaluation of cultural brokenness, or even the daily pic of your growing baby. None of these activities are sinful in nature—but your motives may be. Your posts may be driven by praise. Your picture may come with hidden agendas. In those moments, repent. Pray something like this, "God, it doesn't really matter if I offer my opinion. I don't need to put another picture of my kid out on cyberspace. I don't want to be addicted to see how many like it, share it or comment on it. I don't want my heart to need people's praise. I only need your affirmation. Ground me in your love. In Jesus' name. Amen." Daily repentance will grind away at your flesh's need to be known and praised.

WEAKNESS WILL BE YOUR STRENGTH

Second Corinthians 12 is a scary passage. Paul has just finished a long discourse on why he has every right to boast. He is a Hebrew of Hebrews, son of Abraham, he's been shipwrecked, beaten, stoned, and imprisoned all for the sake of Christ. Paul has a Christian resume that would put all of us to shame. And then Paul says, *"I knew a man...."* Lots of theologians think this is code for, "This happened to me, but I'm not going to say it was me because it was too glorious!" But this man, *"was caught up into paradise— whether in the body or out of the body I do not know, God knows— and he heard things that cannot be told, which man may not utter."* (v. 3–4) Paul has every reason to walk in a measure of pride—even a pride that could appear godly in nature. But Paul tell us, *"to keep me from becoming conceited because of the surpassing greatness of the revelations, a thorn was given me in the flesh, a messenger of Satan to harass me, to keep me from becoming conceited."* (v. 9) God is serious about keeping powerful men weak. God may not limit experiences with the Holy Spirit, but he may limit our strength so that we will not become proud of those experiences.

Embrace the weakness that God allows and even brings into your life. God reminded Paul, *"My grace is sufficient for you. In your weakness my power is made perfect."* And that's the goal—Jesus' power and grace getting a platform in your life. He may look good when you are strong, but He will look most attractive when you are fully dependent on Him in your weakness.

BE QUIET

Stop talking. Practice humility by being quiet. *2 Timothy 2:16 says, "Avoid godless [chatter], because those who indulge in it become more and more ungodly."* (NIV) Have you ever considered that your many words are causing you to drift from God's heart? Often the more we talk, the more we find our language to be about us.

Solomon knew this when he said, *"When there are many words, sin is not far behind" (NIV)* (Proverbs 10:19). So just keep that hole in your face closed. I know you have a funny story to tell. I know your opinion and advice would be well received in this moment. I know that he is deceived and you need to bring correction. I get it! You're awesome. But maybe the best thing you can do is just listen for a change. Perhaps the best thing you and I can do is slow things down and remember God is in charge. Psalm 46:10 reminds us, ""Be still, and know that I am God." Good advice. But why? What's the end game for God in that we be still and know He is God? "I will be exalted among the nations, I will be exalted in the earth!" The answer? So God can be lifted up. God's design in your quiet is so he can get the applause, the laugh, the credit and the worship.

NO MORE SELF-PROMOTION

This daily practice is a second cousin to being quiet, but it takes it a step further. It's one thing to be silent when nothing is riding on your words except maybe a quick laugh or a pat on the back, but what about when your words, stories, quirky yarns, and even tall tales are said because ultimately they may serve you? What about when you need a job or a promotion, and the only way to be recognized is by promoting yourself? Is it possible to pursue a life of humility, background living and glory-giving and still promote yourself? I contend with you—*no!* The moment we begin to advertise our own agenda, giftings, rights and success is the moment we have fallen into the neighborhood of self-promotion. When lucrative salaries and standard of living is at stake, I recognize the difficulty of making war on this area of your heart. But it is necessary to root out every area of pride.

How does this work? God has promised His people that He will provide for their needs. We work an honest day respecting and honoring our employer, honoring God with our time and craft, and believing that God will provide for our needs. Any more than that may be a godless ambition.

Whole books have been written on the subject of ambition, promoting self while not looking like an arrogant jerk, and the like. But it feels a bit disingenuous to say, "God is in control. I don't have to make a name for myself. I don't have to get the credit," and then at the same time making work an idol by giving our best affection to a project and getting our name out there.

1 Thessalonians 4:11 is my go-to whenever ungodly ambition raises it nasty head in my life: *"Make it your ambition to lead a quiet life: You should mind your own business and work with your hands...." (NIV)* It appears that God isn't as interested in you and me moving up the ladder as we'd like to think. I love that the command actually uses the word "ambition." Is Paul trying to be ironic? Either way, with all the energy you would normally use to move up, use all that energy to go down. Make it your ambition to get low, fade into the background, and see how God might shine.

SERVE YOUR CHURCH

There is something pure about serving when it doesn't benefit us at all. When our hands are put to work in furthering the mission of something larger than us, it reminds us that this life isn't about us. Make serving your church family a part of your natural rhythm. Volunteer to teach children every weekend the beautiful story of Jesus. Be a smiling face at the front door. Hand out groceries in an impoverished neighborhood. Take a meal to a family that is grieving. God has put you where you are with the people you worship with so that you might serve them.

This last week Jill, a woman in our church, called our children's director just to ask if we needed some help during Easter. She knows that our children's ministry already requires a truckload of volunteers to shepherd our children, but she knew Easter would require even more. With no prompting, Jill called and asked, "How can I serve? What can I do to help? This is my church, too!" Like everyone else, Jill wanted to be in church for Easter. But serving is part of her DNA as a disciple. She got low so that Jesus could be lifted high in our kindergarten class. As I was sitting in the sanctuary with my family singing the songs of resurrection, I became a bit emotional knowing that Jill was modeling the life of Jesus in a profound way.

AFTERTHOUGHTS

This weekend I'm a retreatant at a Catholic monastery. I am neither Catholic nor good at retreating. But nonetheless my wife informed me my heart seemed to be growing cold to her and to others, and perhaps I needed a few days away. She has always been my greatest counselor. She is warm and firm at the same time. Holding punches has never been her forte, but I usually end up thanking her from behind the black eye she gave me. So I am sitting most of these days watching these nuns do their work. To be fair I'm not exactly sure what nuns do. I assumed they spent their days making wine or cheese or praying for hours in Latin. I don't know. But I have watched them come and go from their jobs. And they do have jobs. Some are weeding a garden, others are in the kitchen, and I saw a dangerous-looking nun getting on a tractor. No habits at this monastery. Jeans and t-shirts are the apparent dress code. And I have been caught off guard by how "every day" these women are. *Ordinary* is the word that comes to mind. I know that sounds pedantic or condescending. I don't mean it that way. I just mean that these are women of routine. They have their jobs and responsibilities just like me, but also a depth of humility I don't see very often, especially in myself. These women have chosen a rhythm of humility. Instead of high highs and low lows, these women have chosen a life that has a much thicker middle than highs or lows. This routine looks almost the same every day. How it works is they work, pray, eat, work, pray, eat, work, pray, eat. It sounds eerily familiar to my life except I don't do that much praying. I work, eat, work, work, eat, sleep, eat, eat, eat and then pray. These nuns, along with other retreatants like myself, are invited into the rhythm of prayer and submission to the Lord. We wake up and there are morning prayers in the chapel. Chanting is involved so it's kind of cool. Then we are released to go and walk, read, enjoy a conversation, and then invited back to noon prayer. After lunch the routine resumes and we are again invited to night prayer and then a meal in silence. And that's the routine. Everyday. I will leave here in a couple of days, but I will miss the predictable environment that my soul has come to expect. I will miss the routine of laying myself down before the Lord regardless of how I feel or what I am thinking or whatever anxiety I am battling with. This habit of getting low is doing something in my heart.

Is there any reason why you and I can't have regular times to reset our hearts? You don't have to go away for a few days or even be Catholic to regularly submit your heart to God. Turn off the TV, close down your computer, and put your phone in a drawer. Kneel down at your bed and get low. Start there. End there. I really believe in those moments we see our lives for what they are—moments of grace, lived in the light of the grandeur and majesty of God. And maybe you and I will breathe a prayer of humility confessing that He is in control and He carries the weight of this life and the next.